ONE MILLION

ONE MILLION

Hendrik Hertzberg

T I M E S 🆃 B O O K S

R A N D O M H O U S E

All rights reserved under International and Pan-American Copyright
Conventions. Published in the United States by Times Books, a division of
Random House, Inc., New York, and simultaneously in Canada by Random
House of Canada Limited, Toronto.

Library of Congress Cataloging-in-Publication Data

Hertzberg, Hendrik.
    One million / by Hendrik Hertzberg.
        p.   cm.
    ISBN 0-8129-2099-6
    1. Million (The number)   I. Title.
    QA141.H47 1993
    513.2'11—dc20   92-56819

Designed by Michael Mendelsohn and Susannah Ing

Manufactured in the United States of America

9 8 7 6 5 4 3 2

First Edition

For Triny

ACKNOWLEDGMENTS

For research help that was witty as well as resourceful, I'm grateful to my friends Daisy Voigt, Anna Husarska, and Michele Slung. Thanks also to Bradley Smith, who got the joke of this book before anyone else, and to Esther Newberg, Steve Wasserman, and Sara Mosle for various forms of encouragement and support.

How big is a million? Big. Oh, you want me to be specific? All right, then: see pages 1 through 200.

The plan of this book (if this is a book) is simple. Five thousand dots to a page—ten thousand on each double-page spread. Two hundred pages. One million dots, not counting the period at the end of this sentence. (And the one at the end of this sentence. And this one. Etcetera.)

The progression is marked at the top of each page. Notes are scattered here and there in the inside margins like billboards along a highway. Each note corresponds to a number, and the dot signifying that number is printed in red.

When the marginal notes refer to events in historical time, the scale is usually measured in days. Conveniently, most of recorded history has taken place within the past one million days. The first dot represents January 1, 1993, and the number sequence moves back from there, through the world wars, the Industrial Revolution, the Middle Ages, Imperial Rome, the birth of the Buddha, and beyond. The millionth dot, by the way, represents March 25, 745 B.C.

When the notes refer to the present time, the figures are the latest available, or are drawn from a typical year in the last decade, whichever is appropriate.

One million is a pretty big number. But in a world of five and a half billion souls, even a million can be a trifling quantity. In some of the notes, therefore, each dot stands for a thousand; in others, each dot itself stands for a million.

The facts herein are drawn from many sources, all of which I believe to be reliable. However, under no circumstances should this book be mistaken for a reference work. Unlike the plastic bags your dry cleaning comes back in, this book *is* a toy. But it is a toy with an earnest purpose, like one of those anatomically correct dolls. Besides being, I hope, fun, it is meant to be an aid to comprehension.

As you riffle slowly through these pages you will see with your own eyes precisely what is meant by one million. If you've just heard on the radio that a million people have been left homeless in a storm, a few moments with this book in your hands will more fully acquaint you with the dimensions of that disaster. If you're wondering what it would be like to be a millionaire, look at the first few pages (representing, if you're lucky, your own bank account) and then flip enviously through the rest. If you're curious about those five and a half billion souls, imagine 5,500 copies of this book (better still, buy them). That many copies would take up about 150 linear feet of shelf space—enough to fill six standard freestanding bookshelves.

Every day, the newspaper and your ingenuity will provide reasons to consult this book. You may wish to scribble information in the margins marking pertinent events and odd discoveries of your own. Or you may prefer simply to give some thought to a quantity, one million, that is almost always taken for granted—and, while you're at it, to contemplate (*a*) the greatness of the Earth and its inhabitants, and then (*b*) the pathetic puniness of our planet and its people next to the vastness of the universe.

NUMBERS AND THEIR NAMES

Humankind is a symbol-making species. Certainly our talent for naming things exceeds our capacity for understanding them. Everyone knows the names of infinity, eternity, truth, and God; few people, if any, know what these things are. Naming a thing is often a substitute for knowing what it actually is, and in some instances a rather good substitute at that. This is certainly the case with numbers. We know the names of the big numbers. We know how to work with the symbols we have made for them. We may not understand their amplitude, but we manipulate them with blithe insouciance. Ten million times ten million? A hundred thousand billion. Next problem, please.

Knowing the name—spoken or written—of a number is not the same as understanding it or knowing how to use it, but it is a prerequisite to both. Among certain preliterate peoples, there are only four number names: *one, two, three,* and *many.* Someone from such a society would be hard put to distinguish between a pile of five objects and a pile of ten, a circumstance on which traders have grown rich. In Western languages, the available words for big numbers are not very . . . well, not very numerous. The everyday English of the prescientific age had *dozen, score, gross, hundred, thousand,* and *myriad* (which technically means ten thousand but was always more commonly understood to mean simply a lot). This vocabulary of quantity sufficed for a time and place in which the Earth was believed to be the center of the universe, which itself was thought to be rather small and only a few thousand years old.

As for the word *million,* it is of comparatively recent coinage. The English word comes to us via the French, who got it from the Romans. It combines *mille,* which means a thousand in both Latin and French, with *-ion,* which lexicographers call an "augmentative suffix." The editors of the *Oxford English Dictionary* found uses of the English word *hundred* as far back as the year A.D. 950, but *million* doesn't make its first known written appearance until four centuries later, in a 1362 manuscript that speaks of "Milions more of Men and of Wymmen." The word reappears about a decade later, in a religious poem about "a Milioun Angeles." Chaucer too wrote of angels, "many a Millioun" of them. In the King James Bible (1611), the brothers of Abraham's bride address her as follows: "And they blessed Rebekah, and said unto her, Thou art our sister, be thou the mother of thousands of millions, and let thy seed possess the gate of those which hate them" (Genesis 24:60). In *Hamlet,* the prince, telling the play-within-the-play actors about a theater piece that apparently went over big with the critics but was box-office poison, says, "The play, I remember, pleased not the million."

Shakespeare, Chaucer, and the biblical scribe were neither the first nor the last writers of English to use the word *million* hyperbolically. Its use in the precise numerical sense—a thousand thousand, ten to the sixth power—became common in the West only in the past couple of centuries. In the East, however, even ancient mythology deals in ages of hundreds of millions of years, and the business of number-naming made considerable progress at an early date. "The time and number sense of the ancient Indians was extraordinary," writes Jawaharlal Nehru, modern India's first prime minister, in *The Discovery of India.* "They had a long series of number names for very high numerals. The Greeks, Romans, Persians, and Arabs had apparently no terminology for denominations above the thousand or at most the myriad (10^4 = 10,000). In India there were eighteen specific denominations (10^{18}) and there are even longer lists. In the story of Buddha's early education he is reported to have named denominations up to 10^{50}"—that is, up to the number we would represent by a one followed by fifty zeros.

Twentieth-century scientific discoveries have forced us in the West to concern ourselves with the kinds of numbers the Buddha named (and possibly even understood). There is, of course, no such thing as "the biggest number in the world"—our number system is open-ended, and another zero can always be added. If we let *n* stand for the biggest number in the world, some wiseacre will always be on hand to point out that *n* + 1 is ever so slightly bigger. The largest number that has a one-word name, however, is the googolplex.

A googolplex is ten carried to the power of a googol, or the numeral 1 followed by a googol of zeros . . . but this is unhelpful. A googol, which stands in relation to a googolplex as a gnat to the galaxy, is itself (despite the cuteness of its name, which was coined by a nine-year-old boy) a very large number. It is 10^{100}, ten to the hundredth power—ten multiplied by itself a hundred times, or, written out in the conventional manner,

10,000,000,000,000,000,000,000,000,000,000,000,000,000,000,000,000,000,000,-000,000,000,000,000,000,000,000,000,000,000,000,000,000,000. This number is, as the saying goes, big enough for all practical purposes. It is so big, in fact, that it is a million, million, billion times larger than the number of all the electrons in the universe (estimated at 10^{79} by Sir Arthur Eddington). (This is the main reason that the plan for a sequel to this book titled *One Googol,* containing a googol of dots, has had to be dropped.)

A googolplex, to repeat, is 10 to the googolth power, or 1 followed by a googol of zeros. Thanks to the genius who hit upon the idea of writing large numbers as exponents of ten, a googolplex can be expressed quite concisely as $10^{10^{googol}}$ or $10(10^{10})$. This looks innocuous, but actually it is a number so colossally huge, so monstrously stupendous, so titanically gargantuan, that it renders trivial anything in human or galactic experience. Not that the googolplex is entirely without its uses. For instance, Edward Kasner and James Newman, the authors of *Mathematics and the Imagination,* once asked themselves how long it would take a book to jump up into your hand if you held it patiently on the end of a string. This odd event would come to pass if all the air molecules on the underside of the book, in their random movements, happened to bump into it at the same instant. "The right answer," Kasner and Newman concluded, "is that it will almost certainly happen sometime in less than a googolplex of years—perhaps tomorrow." So even a googolplex can have an application, though it would be stretching a point to call it a "practical" application.

Naturally, there can be no question of accumulating a googolplex of objects, since that many objects do not, so far as is known, exist. Even with inflation and/or a king-size cut in the capital gains tax, no one is going to become a googolplexaire. Nor, come to think of it, would it be possible to write out a googolplex in full as we wrote out a googol above, for if every book ever printed—not only here on Earth but on all the hundred trillion planets in the universe that many astronomers now believe harbor higher civilizations—were filled with zeros from cover to cover, the resulting number, while undeniably large, would still add up to only a few million trillionths of a googolplex. (Compared to the infinite, of course, even a googolplex is infinitely small.)

We owe our ability to write big numbers on small pieces of paper to an unknown but very smart resident of India, who, at about the time of the birth of Christ, invented the zero and the place-value system. These advances simplified number-writing in the same way that the phonetic alphabet simplified word-writing. Roman numerals, with which teachers have tormented their pupils for centuries, are clumsy not because they use M's and X's instead of 5's and 6's, but because they do not know how to multiply their value by changing their position.

Our own number system happens to be based on ten, which means that each time a numeral gets nudged one place to the left, its value increases ten times. The number 9,482, for instance, is just a shorthand way of writing 9,000 plus 400 plus 80 plus 2, or to put it another way, 2 plus 8×10 plus 4×10^2 plus 9×10^3. The fact that this system is decimal (that is, based on ten) is a biological coincidence. If we had six fingers on each hand, we would undoubtedly now be counting by twelves. In that case, the numeral one-zero (10) would have the value of twelve, and we would have to invent new single-place symbols for the values of ten and eleven (B and C would do nicely). We would then write the numbers for one through twenty-four this way: 1, 2, 3, 4, 5, 6, 7, 8, 9, B, C, 10, 11, 12, 13, 14, 15, 16, 17, 18, 19, 1B, 1C, 20. Actually, this system would have distinct advantages, since twelve is evenly divisible by one, two, three, four, six, and itself, while ten is divisible only by one, two, five, and itself.

There is nothing holy about ten, but all of us are so conditioned to thinking in tens that it is difficult to think about numbers in any other terms. We regard ten and its multiples (hundreds, thousands, millions) as somehow special, as mileposts on the turnpikes of quantity. And they are mileposts, but only in our minds, not in nature. Another little foray into the twelve-based number system will show just how arbitrary our ten-minded system is. In the twelve-based system, the figure 1,000,000 would have the value (and here we must suddenly shift back to "regular" numbers) of 12^6, or 2,985,584. The figure 1,000,000,000 would have the value of 5,159,780,352. Conversely, "our" one million would be expressed, in twelve-based numbers, as 412,160; "our" one billion would be expressed as 23B,B93,4B8. If the medieval Church had wanted to avoid all the hysteria surrounding the dawning of the millennium, it could simply have decreed that henceforth the number system would be based on twelve; then the year "1000" would not have rolled around until 1728, by which time the Enlightenment had things well in hand. (And we wouldn't have to worry about "the year 2000" until A.D. 3456.)

Too much shifting back and forth between number systems can get vexing, like trying to switch a full-size train onto a narrow-gauge track. To avoid mental derailments, it pays to stick to just one system. But the process of switching around is really not so different from switching between the Celsius and Fahrenheit temperature scales, say, or the English and metric systems of measuring distance. The boiling point of water stays the same whether you call it 100 degrees or 212. The distance from New York to California stays the same whether you call it 3,000 (miles) or 5,000 (kilometers); and the number of days in a year stays the same, too, whether you write it as 365 or (in the twelve-based system) as 265.

Computers, which are rather stupid in certain ways, have to use a number system based on two. Their system uses only two symbols, 0 and 1, and each time a digit moves to the left, it gets multiplied by two instead of by ten. So a computer counts to ten this way: 1, 10, 11, 100, 101, 110, 111, 1000, 1001, 1010. We would find this system tiresome; the numbers, especially the big ones, run on and on. In computer numbers, there are 101,101,101 days in a year, and "one million" looks like this: 11,110,100,001,000,000. But computers seem to like it this way, because they only know how to count to two anyway (a switch is either on or off), and because, despite the endless digits, these "binary" numbers actually require fewer choices. A computer has to make only forty choices to write the number one million—twenty digits, two possible symbols per digit. We have to make seventy choices—seven digits, ten symbols. Maybe computers aren't as dumb as they look.

BIG, YES, BUT HOW BIG?

"I have measured out my life in coffee spoons."
—T. S. Eliot

As a unit of measurement, the coffee spoon happens to lie midway between the very small and the very large. The length of a coffee spoon is, for example, about one thousand times greater than that of a grain of sand, and about one-thousandth the height of a skyscraper. It is a hundred million times longer than a sugar molecule, and a hundred million times shorter than the diameter of the Earth. It is a trillion times as long as an electron, and a trillion times smaller than the distance from the Earth to the Sun.

Technically, I know, it is man, not his coffee spoons, who is the measure of all things. And he is happily situated to do the measuring. (She is, too, of course. That goes without saying.) He is not so big as to ignore the little things, like the bacteria living in his intestines (to whom he is the size of the Earth), the atoms of which he is made (in comparison to which he is as large as the solar system), and the protons in the nuclei of those atoms (next to which his height is roughly equal to the distance to Alpha Centauri, the nearest bright star). Yet he is not so small that his sense organs, and their optical and electronic extensions, cannot perceive something of the enormity of the cosmos. And his brain is so flexible and powerful that it can map the molecules of its own genetic code and plot the chemistry of stars in distant galaxies.

Lest we grow too impressed with ourselves, however, it is well to recall the physical insignificance of ourselves and our little planet in the larger scheme of things. If, for example, the Earth is imagined to be the size of a golf ball, the Sun would be a sphere twenty feet in diameter, and it would be nearly a half mile away. If the solar system were the size of a golf ball, the Sun would be visible only under a microscope. The nearest star would be two hundred yards away, and the breadth of our galaxy, the Milky Way, would be some 2,600 miles, about the distance between New York and Mexico City. If the galaxy were the size of a golf ball, the solar system would be about as big as a molecule. Other galaxies—peas, marbles, softballs, and soccer balls—would lie here and there, from a yard to several miles away. And here the analogy must stop, for the next question ("What if the whole universe were the size of a golf ball?") is, from any normal person's perspective, absurd. A Zen master, however, would not have a problem with it. Neither would an astronomer interested in cosmology, for if, as much recent research suggests, the universe is closed—meaning it has enough matter in it so that eventually it will stop expanding and will collapse back in on itself—then from the "outside," wherever that is, the universe may well actually *be* the size of a golf ball.

The star we are pleased to call the Sun is huge only from our provincial perspective. If a really big star—say, Epsilon Aurigal B—were suddenly to take the place of the Sun, it would do more than merely engulf the nearer planets; the entire solar system would fit into a tiny sphere at its center, with a diameter less than two-tenths of one percent of that of the whole star. Our Sun is a little less than half again as dense as water; by comparison, the density of a neutron star is so extreme that, if the Sun were to fall into one, it would quickly collapse into a ball just three miles across—about the distance from the downtown end of New York's Central Park to the uptown end. At that density, the entire Earth would take up about as much room as a good-sized suburban house. Black holes, the ultimate result of stars collapsing in on themselves from their own gravitational force, are even more unimaginably dense: it has been calculated that a black hole with the mass of the Earth would be about the size of a chick pea.

Time, like space, is immense, and our perception of it tends to be distorted by the extreme youth of our species, just as our spatial perception is often distorted by our tiny size. The universe is now thought to be some fifteen billion years old, and the Earth has existed for a third of that time. Human beings of one kind or another have been walking around for only about a million years, and man in his present (though not necessarily final) form for a mere thirty-seven thousand years. Recorded history has been incredibly brief—some two million days, a wink in the eye of God. If all the dots in this book are allowed to represent the age of the Earth, then life-forms with more than one cell would not emerge until page 169, and dinosaurs not until the top of page 198. The earliest man appears at the end of the fifth line from the bottom of the last page; all recorded history is represented—over-represented—by the last two dots in the book. Even if the scale is reduced five-thousand-fold, so that each dot represents a year (and the whole book, the life span of mankind), the history of civilization happens on the last two pages, the history of the United States begins five lines from the bottom of the last page, the emergence of the technology that dominates urban life is covered in the last two lines, and the post-Soviet, post–Cold War era begins with the last two dots.

The steady, ticking time of clocks and calendars is one of those convenient lies by which we make life smoother for ourselves; or to put it another way, that kind of time is, like Euclidian geometry and Newtonian physics, one of those models of reality that is true for many places and purposes but not for all. All of us are familiar with the experience of time flowing more slowly or more quickly than the clock tells us; and in science, simple, unitary conceptions of time have been laid to rest by modern physics.

The best known of Einstein's equations established that as matter accelerates it gains in mass; and at speeds approaching that of light—the universal limit, at least in this universe—the gain is enormous. There is another effect: as speed increases, time begins to stretch. Carl Sagan has written of the astonishing effects of acceleration on time. A spaceship moving at a steady acceleration of one gravity (enabling the passengers to feel their normal weight, and their ship to attain a velocity of well over 99 percent of the speed of light) would reach the Andromeda Galaxy, a million light-years distant, in thirty years. Upon their return, the passengers would be sixty years older, but the Earth and its civilization, if either still existed, would have aged two million years in their absence. And such a voyage, in which the travelers would travel in time as well as space, is well within the realm of possibility—perhaps within the next century.

One of the peculiarities of our age is the sensation that everything seems to be increasing exponentially—knowledge, wealth, population. Letting this book represent the population of the world today—that would be some 5,500 souls per dot—then the population at the beginning of history would cover only four pages, and that at the time of the Declaration of Independence only forty. Some 7 percent of all the people who have ever lived are alive right now.

With the increases in population and technology, economic activity, too, has grown hugely. For sheer inflation, Weimar Germany, where a total of 496,585,346,000,000,000 marks found their way into circulation after World War I, is still thought to hold the record. At present, however, no single human conglomeration disposes of as much money as the United States government—about one and a half trillion (or fifteen hundred million) dollars a year. To let this book stand for that budget, each dot must represent a sum of one and a half million dollars. Defense gobbles up about forty pages, health and Social Security around eighty-nine, interest on the national debt around twenty-seven, foreign aid and the space program about two pages each, and the National Endowment for the Arts about twenty-five dots. The president's salary gets a tiny slice of a single dot, like a piece of pie fit for a flea.

We need not look to the heavens, or to the statistical abstracts, to find a multitude of things. Even in daily life, vastness is everywhere. An average sugar bowl contains about 400,000 grains of sugar. A hundred-mile railway trip will take the rider over 316,800 railway ties. A sheep's coat may contain as many as 126,000,000 wool fibers. A visit to the beach discloses numerous grains of sand; at Coney Island, there are said to be a hundred billion billion. A talk on one of the world's half billion telephones will add a few dozen words to the twenty-five million billion or so uttered by humankind since the beginning of time.

A FINAL NOTE

". . . at least a hundred million viewers (worldwide estimate: 750 million) will tune in the Super Bowl . . . 30 million retirees receive Social Security checks each month . . . more than 275,000 refugees . . . 84 million gallons of crude oil . . . $8 billion needed this year . . . more than 350,000 killed . . . fourth-quarter income of $42 million . . ."

And on and on, in the thousands and millions and billions, until the eyes glaze over and the brain tunes out. As it happens, these figures are from the first few pages of a recent edition of the *New York Times;* but in this quantifying age, they could be from any publication or news broadcast, any day, anywhere in the world. Some comprehension of numbers like these is evidently a prerequisite to keeping oneself tolerably well informed, for they are everywhere, amid the tales of war and wealth and horseracing. Their importance goes far beyond that, of course. Without some understanding of huge quantities, much of mankind's accumulated wisdom in fields as varied as physics, astronomy, ecology, population dynamics, and economics is simply inaccessible. Big numbers are as much a part of our lives as our own names, which, indeed, they threaten to replace. My own numbers, assigned to me by various bureaucracies, include 35608, 3595056, and 566796766304876643.

Can we—despite the nonchalance with which such figures are dropped in all sorts of contexts—really understand them? Not very likely, except in the most abstract, nonexperiential way. The largest number of discrete objects of which most of us can form a mental picture is five or six, and even those whose minds are thought to be exceptional cannot do much better. "Nine is about my limit," wrote Arthur C. Clarke, whose portraits of the future have fascinated . . . well, millions of readers. "I can just visualize it by imagining three rows of three objects."

Our comprehension is not, of course, limited absolutely by what we can visualize with eyes closed; through memory and association, we can extend it considerably further. Think of a starry night, or of the experience of being in a big crowd at a football game. There were tens of thousands of people in the football stadium (if it was an average NFL game, there were 60,829, to be precise about it); and the stars in the sky, one would naturally suppose, were far more numerous. Not so: even on the clearest night, far away from city lights, only about 3,000 stars are visible to the naked eye. At this level, precision, and with it comprehension, begins to fade.

To "know" something intellectually and to experience it concretely are two very different things. All of us have had concrete experience with the smaller numbers, the ones and tens and hundreds, even the thousands. Millions are harder to come by. Hence what follows.

ONE MILLION

2—Population of the Garden of Eden.

4,435—Americans killed in the Revolutionary War. (See also pages 3, 27, 59, 73, and 82.)

483—The size of Alaska, if Rhode Island equals 1.

1,860—Steps to the 102nd and top floor of the Empire State Building, New York City.

9,602—People killed by handguns in the United States, 1988–90 (as against 46 in Japan and 8 in Canada).

5,790—Languages and dialects spoken by the people of the world.

8,325—Feathers on a Plymouth Rock hen (versus 940 on a ruby-throated hummingbird and 25,216 on a whistling swan).

8,399—Number of times Babe Ruth officially went to bat. (Adding up his singles, doubles, triples, and home runs, he scored 5,793 bases.)

9,850—To 1, the odds of a European woman's dying in pregnancy (as against 6,366 to 1 in the United States and 21 to 1 in Africa).

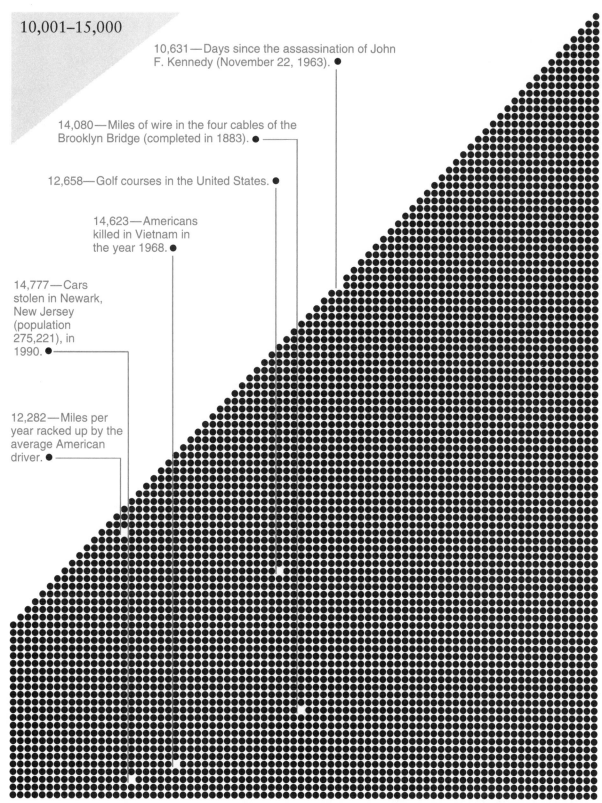

10,631—Days since the assassination of John F. Kennedy (November 22, 1963). ●

14,080—Miles of wire in the four cables of the Brooklyn Bridge (completed in 1883). ●

12,658—Golf courses in the United States. ●

14,623—Americans killed in Vietnam in the year 1968. ●

14,777—Cars stolen in Newark, New Jersey (population 275,221), in 1990. ●

12,282—Miles per year racked up by the average American driver. ●

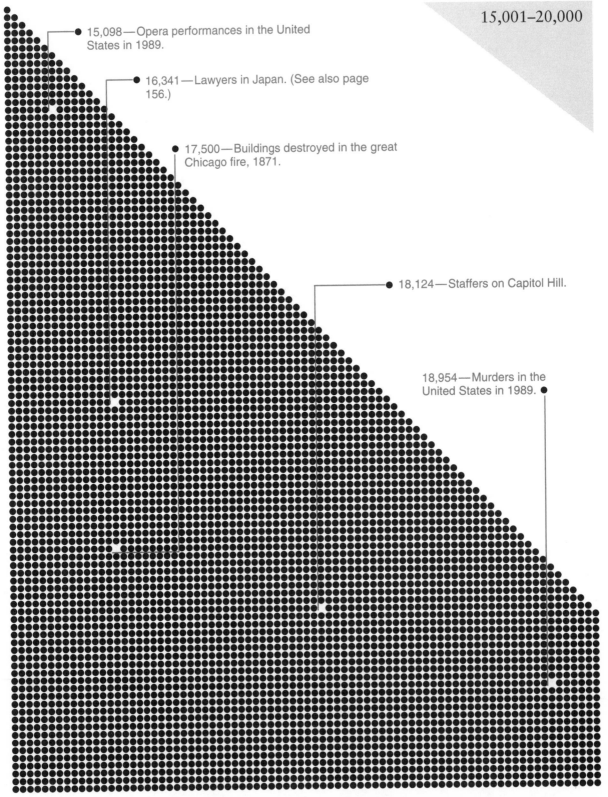

15,098—Opera performances in the United States in 1989.

16,341—Lawyers in Japan. (See also page 156.)

17,500—Buildings destroyed in the great Chicago fire, 1871.

18,124—Staffers on Capitol Hill.

18,954—Murders in the United States in 1989.

20,001–25,000

20,088—Estimated calls per year to 1-800-CALL SPY, a U.S. Army hot line set up to receive reports of espionage. ●

23,148—Phone calls per second dialed by Americans. ●

21,985—Americans used guns to commit suicide in 1988. (Poison—5,825 deaths—was the next most popular method.) (See also page 7.) ●

25,452—Size of the "cast of thousands" of the movie *Ben Hur*.

27,722—Days, the average American's life expectancy at birth.

25,769—Days, the average Russian's life expectancy at birth.

29,551—Words in William Shakespeare's *Hamlet* (as against 29,899 *different* words used by James Joyce in *Ulysses*).

28,124—Days, the average Canadian's life expectancy at birth.

28,709—Days, the average Japanese's life expectancy at birth.

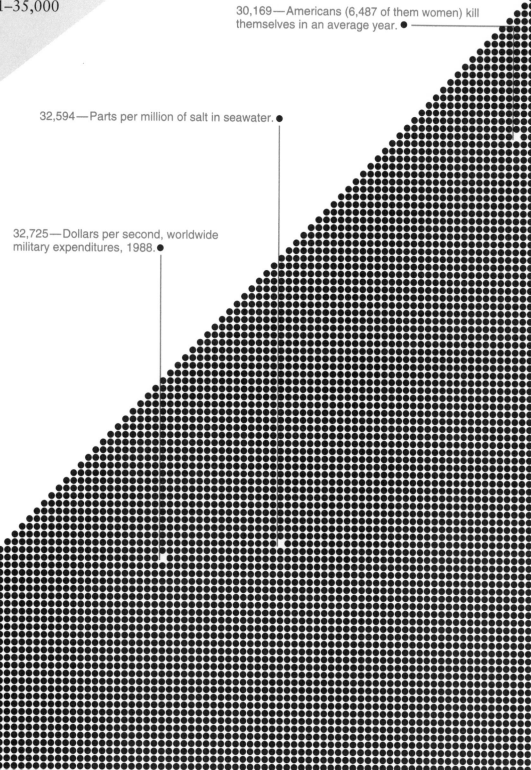

30,169—Americans (6,487 of them women) kill themselves in an average year. ●

32,594—Parts per million of salt in seawater. ●

32,725—Dollars per second, worldwide military expenditures, 1988.●

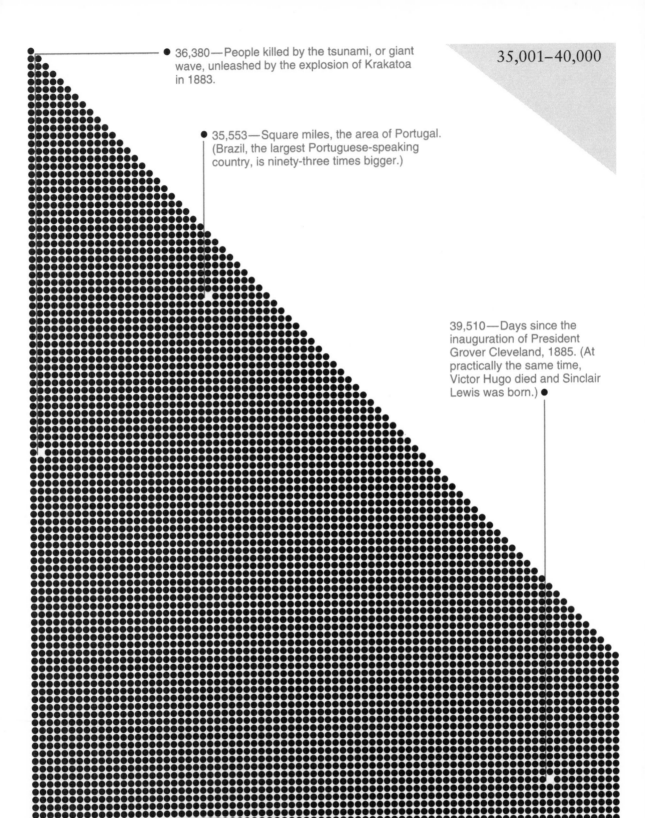

36,380—People killed by the tsunami, or giant wave, unleashed by the explosion of Krakatoa in 1883.

35,553—Square miles, the area of Portugal. (Brazil, the largest Portuguese-speaking country, is ninety-three times bigger.)

39,510—Days since the inauguration of President Grover Cleveland, 1885. (At practically the same time, Victor Hugo died and Sinclair Lewis was born.)

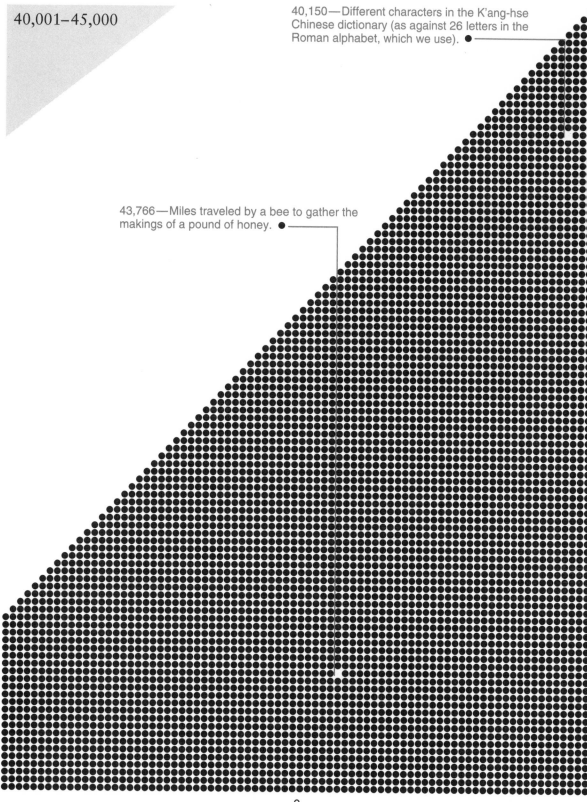

40,150—Different characters in the K'ang-hse Chinese dictionary (as against 26 letters in the Roman alphabet, which we use). ●

43,766—Miles traveled by a bee to gather the makings of a pound of honey. ●

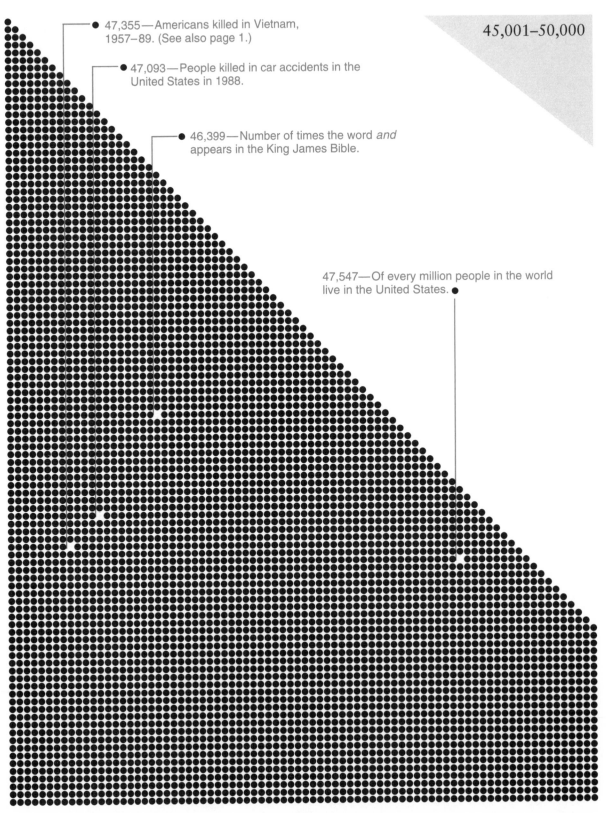

47,355—Americans killed in Vietnam, 1957–89. (See also page 1.)

47,093—People killed in car accidents in the United States in 1988.

46,399—Number of times the word *and* appears in the King James Bible.

47,547—Of every million people in the world live in the United States.

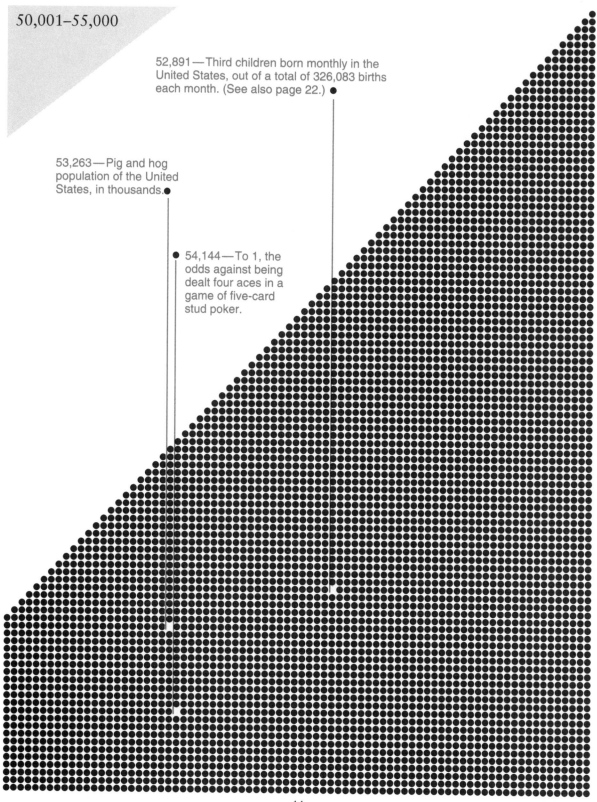

50,001–55,000

52,891—Third children born monthly in the United States, out of a total of 326,083 births each month. (See also page 22.) ●

53,263—Pig and hog population of the United States, in thousands.●

● 54,144—To 1, the odds against being dealt four aces in a game of five-card stud poker.

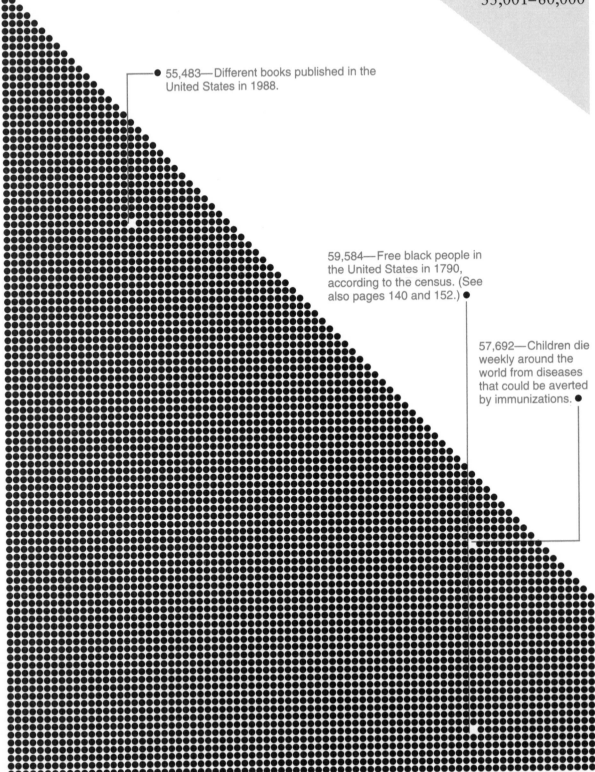

55,483—Different books published in the United States in 1988.

59,584—Free black people in the United States in 1790, according to the census. (See also pages 140 and 152.)

57,692—Children die weekly around the world from diseases that could be averted by immunizations.

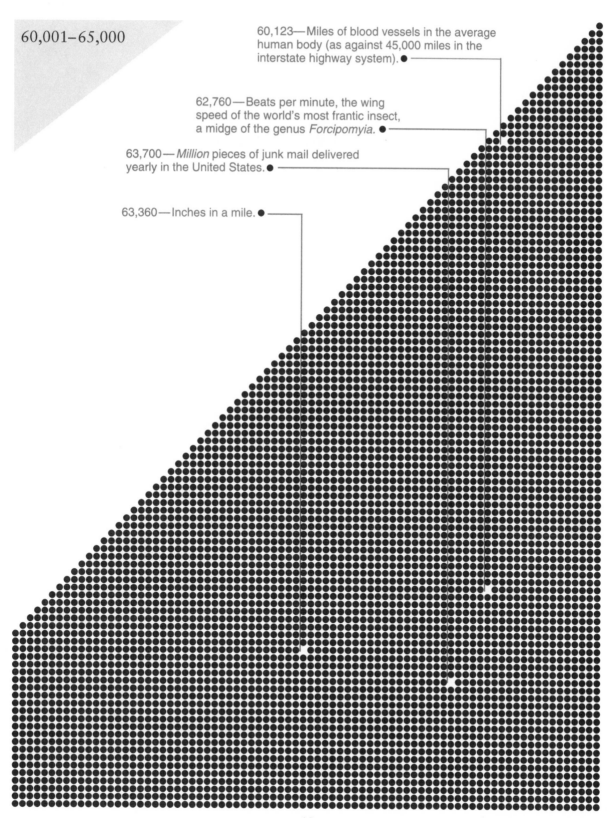

60,123—Miles of blood vessels in the average human body (as against 45,000 miles in the interstate highway system). ●

62,760—Beats per minute, the wing speed of the world's most frantic insect, a midge of the genus *Forcipomyia.* ●

63,700—*Million* pieces of junk mail delivered yearly in the United States. ●

63,360—Inches in a mile. ●

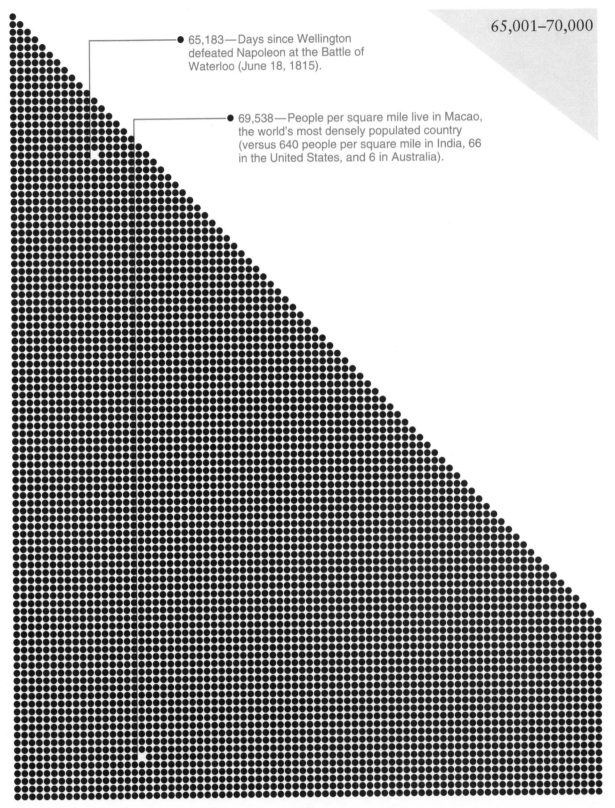

65,183—Days since Wellington defeated Napoleon at the Battle of Waterloo (June 18, 1815).

69,538—People per square mile live in Macao, the world's most densely populated country (versus 640 people per square mile in India, 66 in the United States, and 6 in Australia).

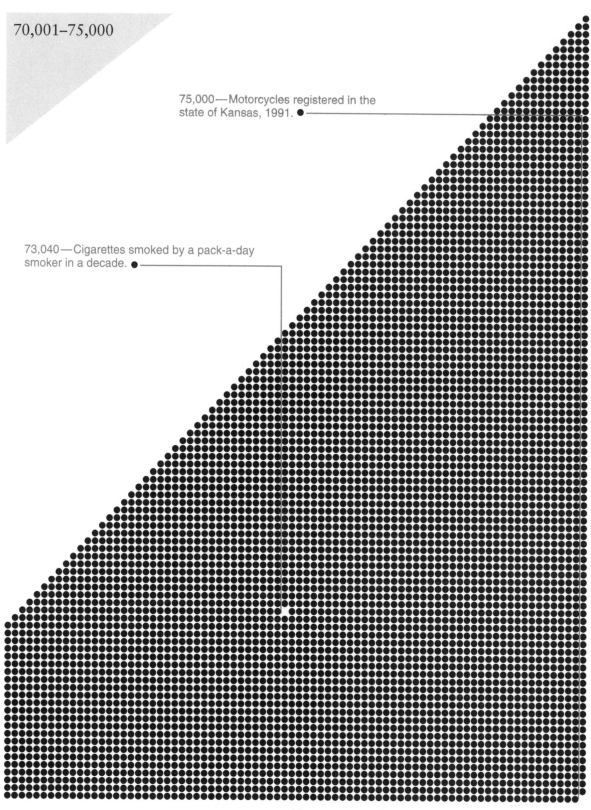

75,000—Motorcycles registered in the state of Kansas, 1991.

73,040—Cigarettes smoked by a pack-a-day smoker in a decade.

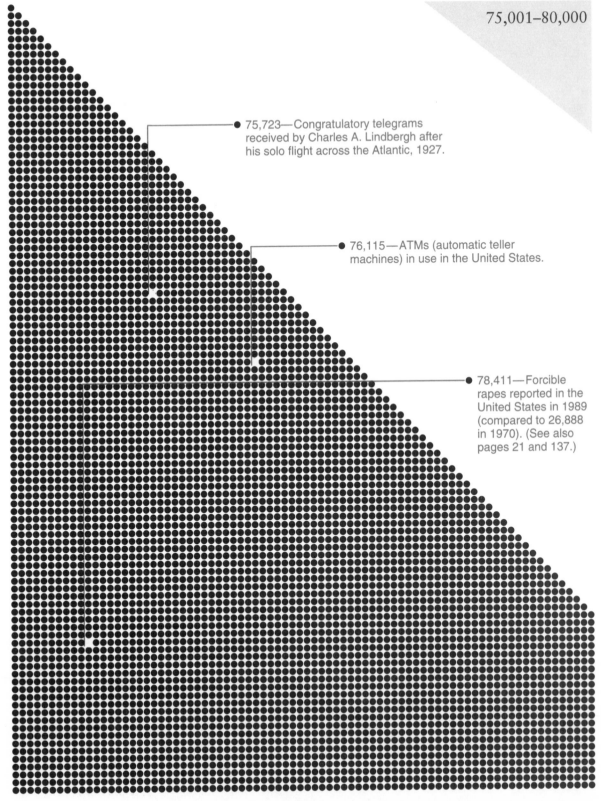

75,723—Congratulatory telegrams received by Charles A. Lindbergh after his solo flight across the Atlantic, 1927.

76,115—ATMs (automatic teller machines) in use in the United States.

78,411—Forcible rapes reported in the United States in 1989 (compared to 26,888 in 1970). (See also pages 21 and 137.)

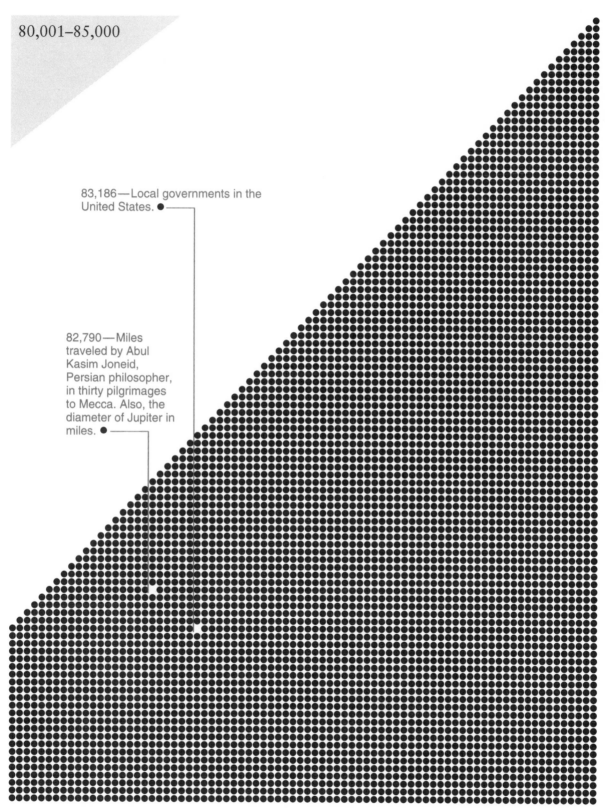

83,186—Local governments in the United States. ●

82,790—Miles traveled by Abul Kasim Joneid, Persian philosopher, in thirty pilgrimages to Mecca. Also, the diameter of Jupiter in miles. ●

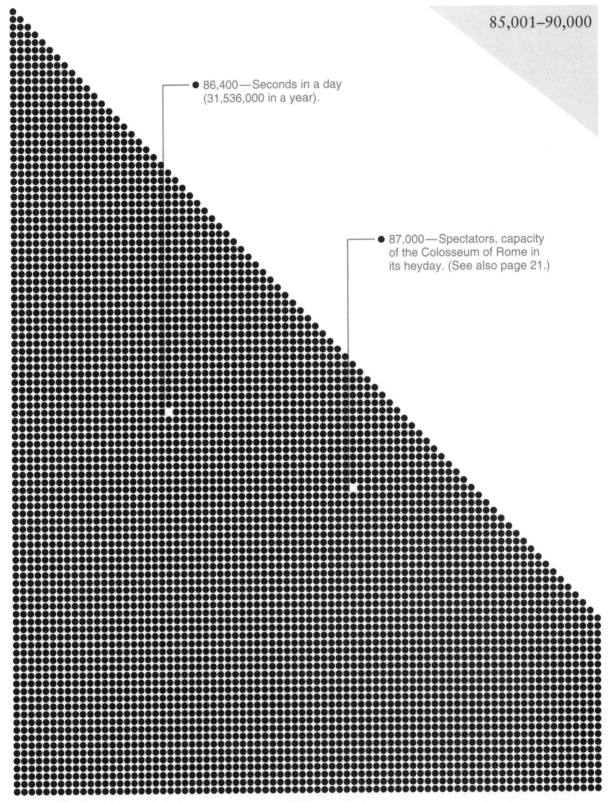

● 86,400—Seconds in a day (31,536,000 in a year).

● 87,000—Spectators, capacity of the Colosseum of Rome in its heyday. (See also page 21.)

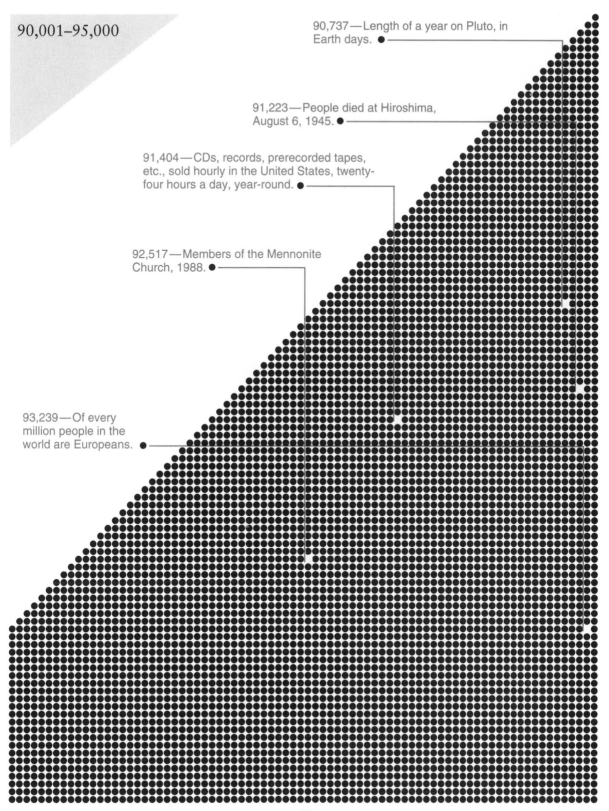

90,737—Length of a year on Pluto, in Earth days. ●

91,223—People died at Hiroshima, August 6, 1945. ●

91,404—CDs, records, prerecorded tapes, etc., sold hourly in the United States, twenty-four hours a day, year-round. ●

92,517—Members of the Mennonite Church, 1988. ●

93,239—Of every million people in the world are Europeans. ●

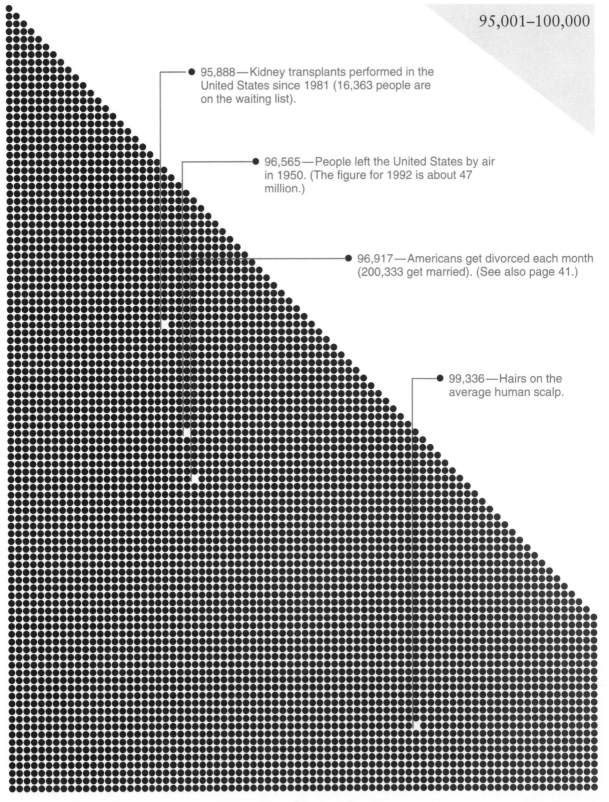

95,888—Kidney transplants performed in the United States since 1981 (16,363 people are on the waiting list).

96,565—People left the United States by air in 1950. (The figure for 1992 is about 47 million.)

96,917—Americans get divorced each month (200,333 get married). (See also page 41.)

99,336—Hairs on the average human scalp.

100,001–105,000

102,555—Rapes reported in the United States in 1990 (more than one every five minutes). ●

100,874—Pounds of food eaten by the average American in a lifetime. ●

102,083—Seats in the Rose Bowl, the largest stadium in the United States. (See also page 18.)

103,255—Native Americans identified Sioux as their tribe in the 1990 Census. (See also page 62.)●

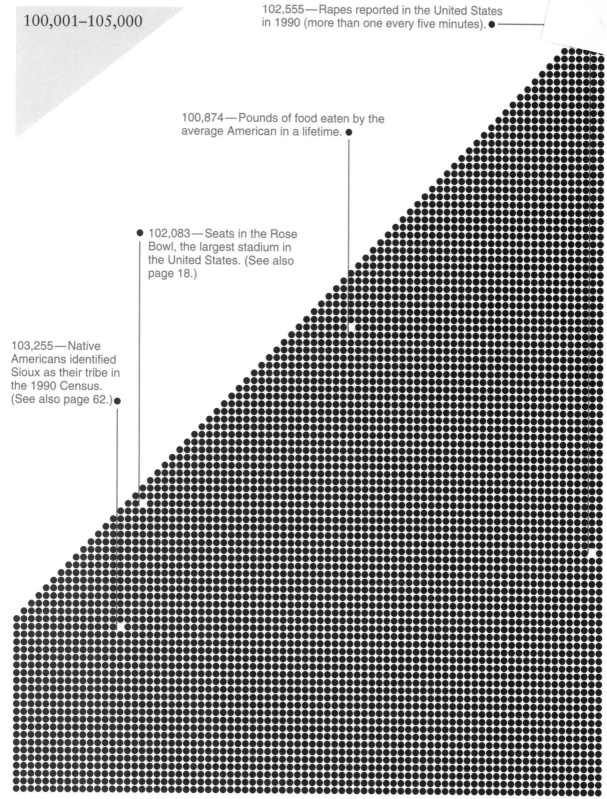

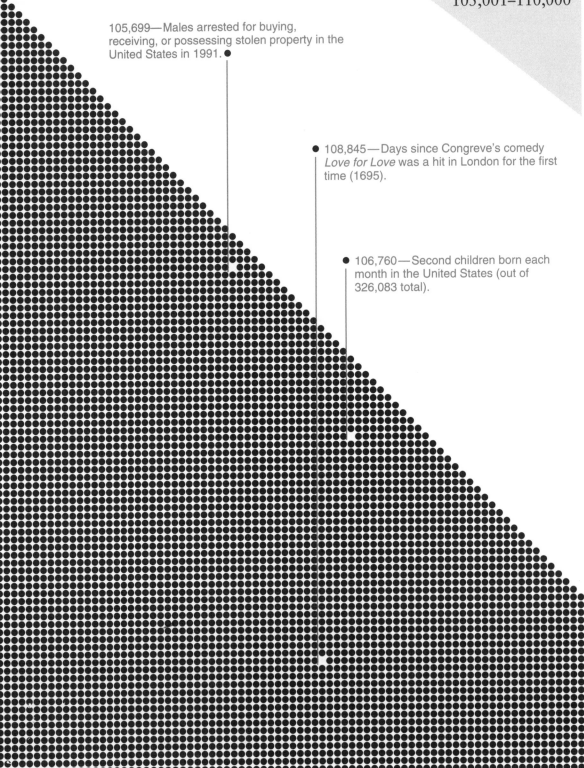

105,699—Males arrested for buying, receiving, or possessing stolen property in the United States in 1991. ●

● 108,845—Days since Congreve's comedy *Love for Love* was a hit in London for the first time (1695).

● 106,760—Second children born each month in the United States (out of 326,083 total).

110,295—Dollars, net worth of Abraham Lincoln at the time of his death, 1865. ●——

112,100—Babies born in 1988 to unmarried Swedish mothers, 50.9 percent of the total number of births in Sweden. (The comparable percentage for the United States was 25.7; for Japan, 1 percent.) ●

● 114,923—Americans injured annually in drinking-glass-related accidents.

● 113,331—Americans injured annually in fence-related accidents (1988).

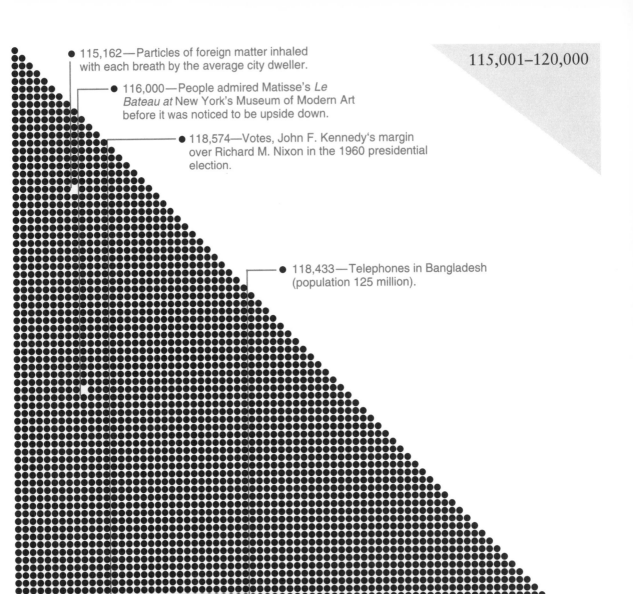

● 115,162—Particles of foreign matter inhaled with each breath by the average city dweller.

● 116,000—People admired Matisse's *Le Bateau at* New York's Museum of Modern Art before it was noticed to be upside down.

● 118,574—Votes, John F. Kennedy's margin over Richard M. Nixon in the 1960 presidential election.

● 118,433—Telephones in Bangladesh (population 125 million).

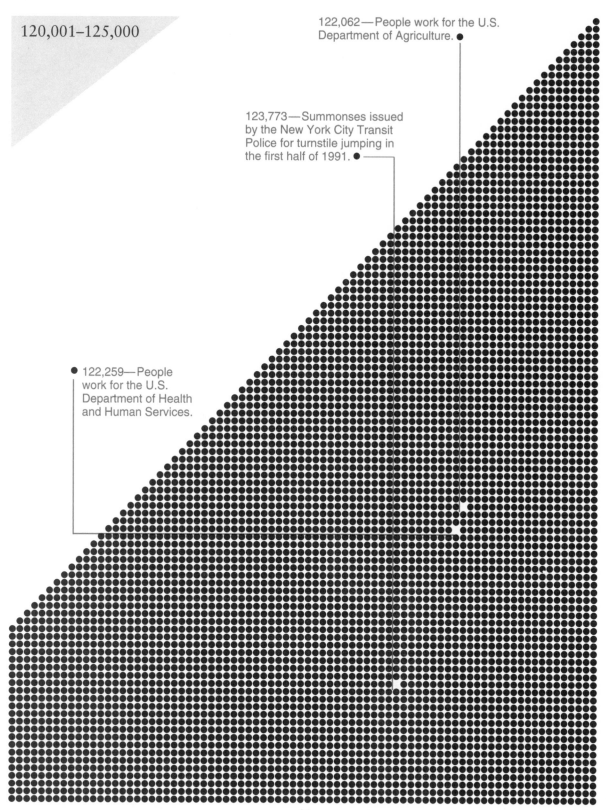

122,062—People work for the U.S. Department of Agriculture.

123,773—Summonses issued by the New York City Transit Police for turnstile jumping in the first half of 1991.

122,259—People work for the U.S. Department of Health and Human Services.

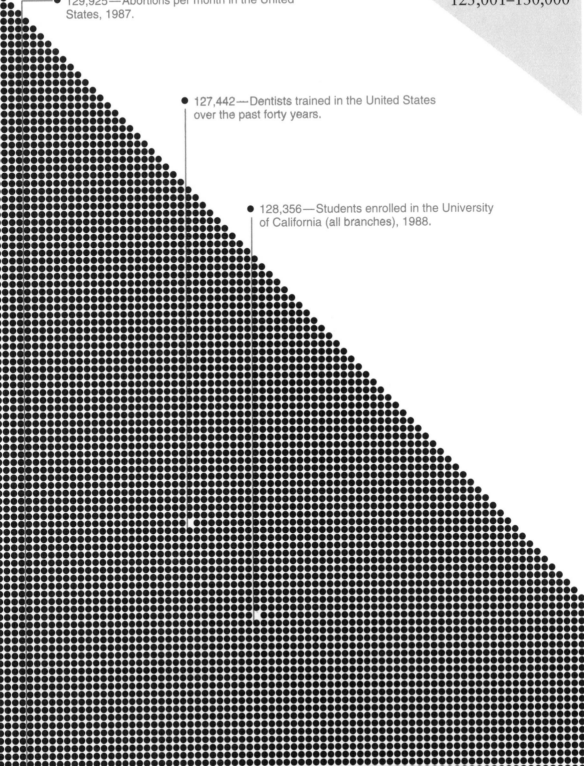

129,925—Abortions per month in the United States, 1987.

125,001–130,000

127,442—Dentists trained in the United States over the past forty years.

128,356—Students enrolled in the University of California (all branches), 1988.

132,000— *Thousand* rods and cones in a pair of human eyes. ●

133,332—People had died of AIDS in the United States as of 1991. (See also pages 41 and 84.)

133,821—Confederate soldiers died in the American Civil War (as against 364,511 Union dead).

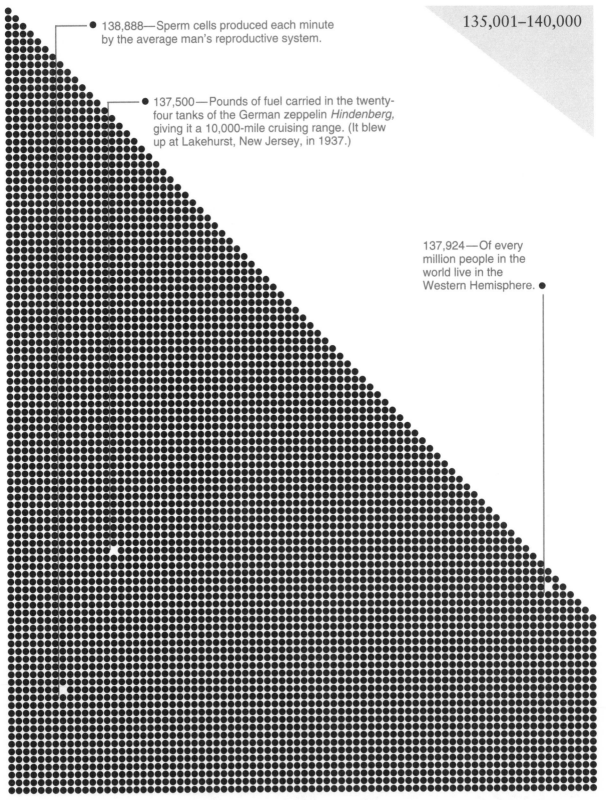

138,888—Sperm cells produced each minute by the average man's reproductive system.

137,500—Pounds of fuel carried in the twenty-four tanks of the German zeppelin *Hindenberg,* giving it a 10,000-mile cruising range. (It blew up at Lakehurst, New Jersey, in 1937.)

137,924—Of every million people in the world live in the Western Hemisphere.

143,550—Square miles, the area of the Caspian Sea, the largest lake in the world (about the size of Japan). (The largest freshwater lake, Lake Superior, is 31,820 square miles.) ●

142,807—People killed by an earthquake at Kwanto Plain, Japan (September 1, 1923). ●

143,352—Dollars, paid for a deck of playing cards by the Metropolitan Museum of Art in 1983. ●

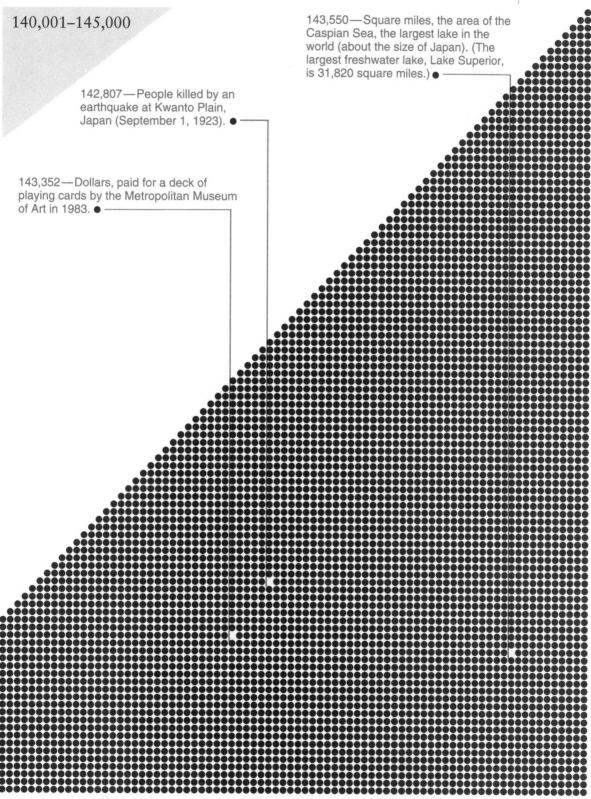

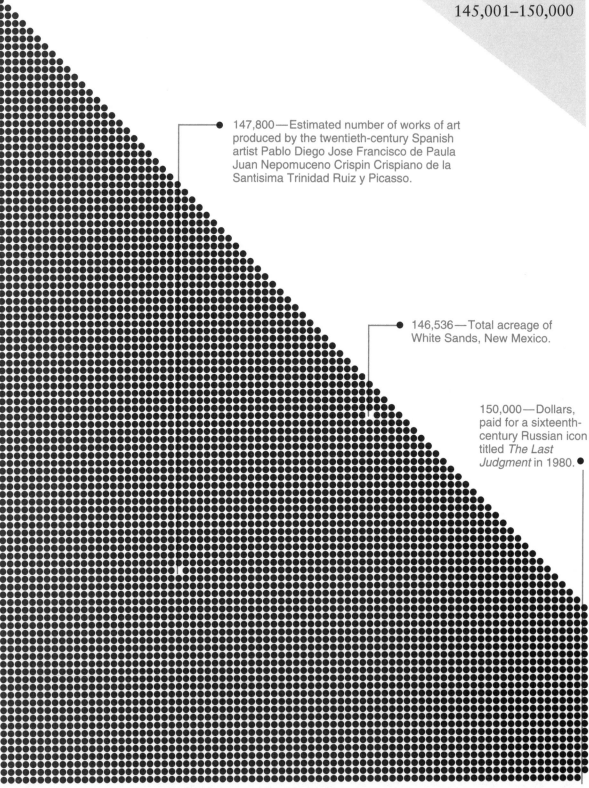

147,800—Estimated number of works of art produced by the twentieth-century Spanish artist Pablo Diego Jose Francisco de Paula Juan Nepomuceno Crispin Crispiano de la Santisima Trinidad Ruiz y Picasso.

146,536—Total acreage of White Sands, New Mexico.

150,000—Dollars, paid for a sixteenth-century Russian icon titled *The Last Judgment* in 1980.

151,164—Items of linen, including 26,200 pillowcases, carried on board the *Queen Elizabeth 2.* ●

154,763—Dollars *per second,* America's gross national product (1988).

153,000—Membership of the International Ladies Garment Workers Union in 1989, down from 363,000 in 1970. ●

153,846—Tickets sold weekly to Broadway shows. ●

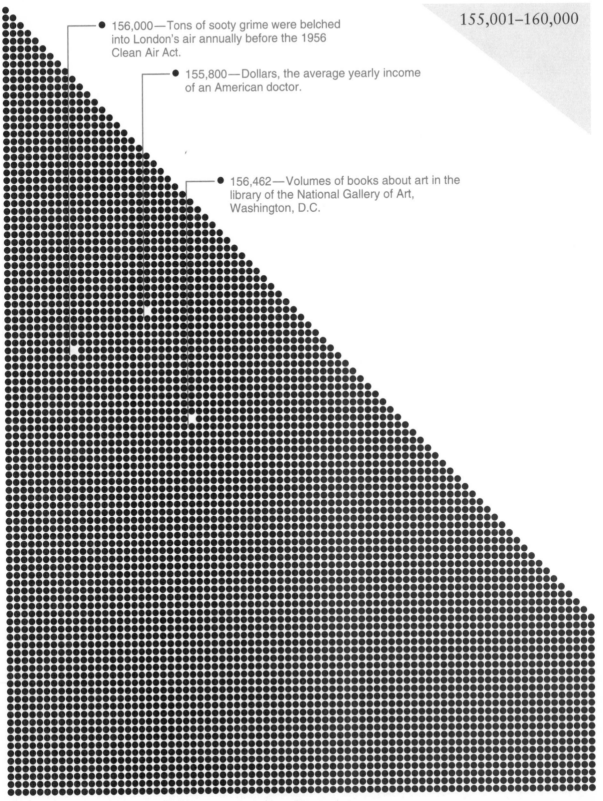

156,000—Tons of sooty grime were belched into London's air annually before the 1956 Clean Air Act.

155,800—Dollars, the average yearly income of an American doctor.

156,462—Volumes of books about art in the library of the National Gallery of Art, Washington, D.C.

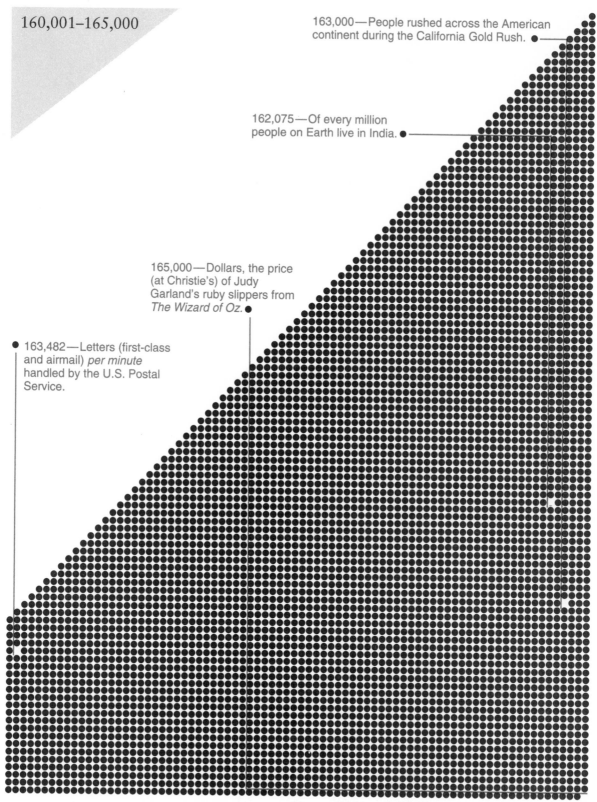

160,001–165,000

163,000—People rushed across the American continent during the California Gold Rush. ●

162,075—Of every million people on Earth live in India. ●

165,000—Dollars, the price (at Christie's) of Judy Garland's ruby slippers from *The Wizard of Oz.* ●

● 163,482—Letters (first-class and airmail) *per minute* handled by the U.S. Postal Service.

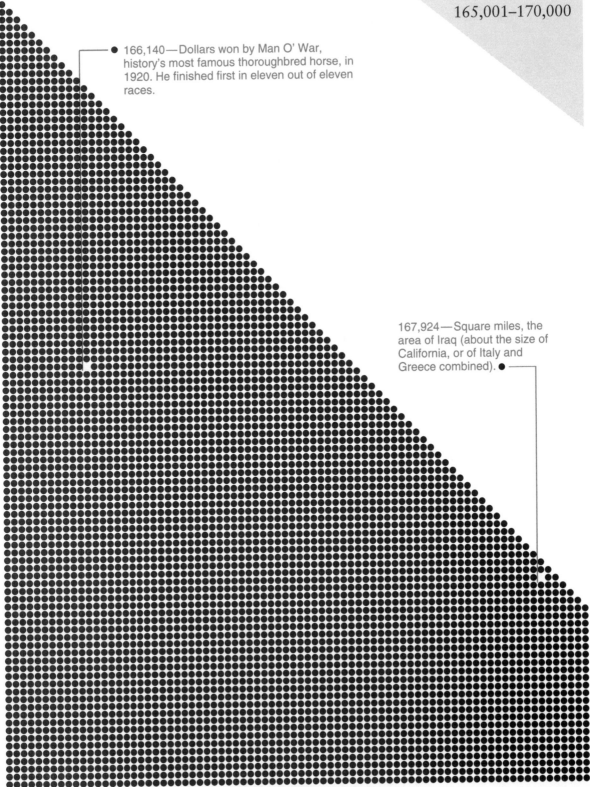

166,140—Dollars won by Man O' War, history's most famous thoroughbred horse, in 1920. He finished first in eleven out of eleven races.

167,924—Square miles, the area of Iraq (about the size of California, or of Italy and Greece combined).

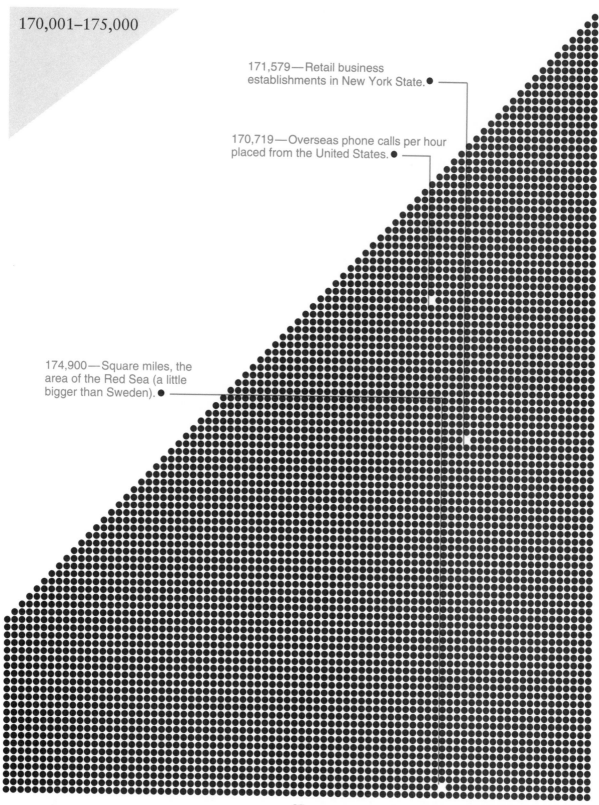

171,579—Retail business establishments in New York State.●

170,719—Overseas phone calls per hour placed from the United States.●

174,900—Square miles, the area of the Red Sea (a little bigger than Sweden).●

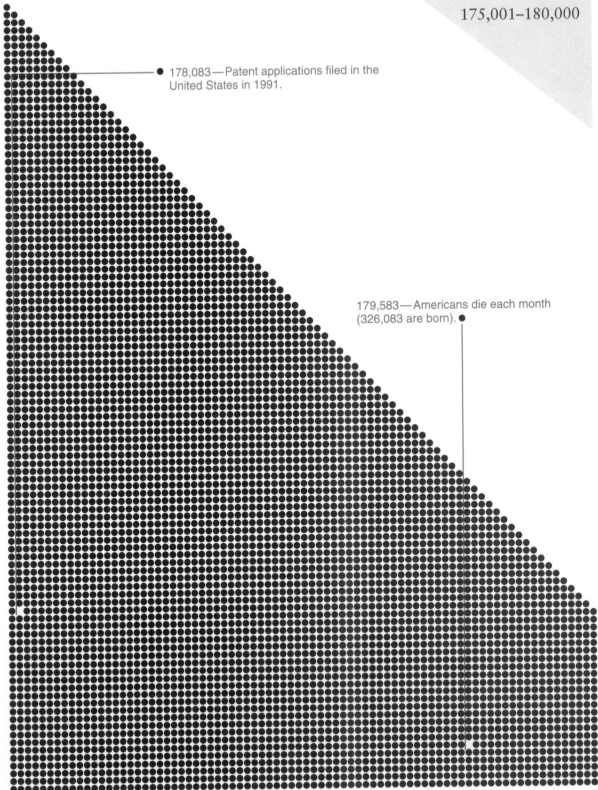

178,083—Patent applications filed in the United States in 1991.

179,583—Americans die each month (326,083 are born).

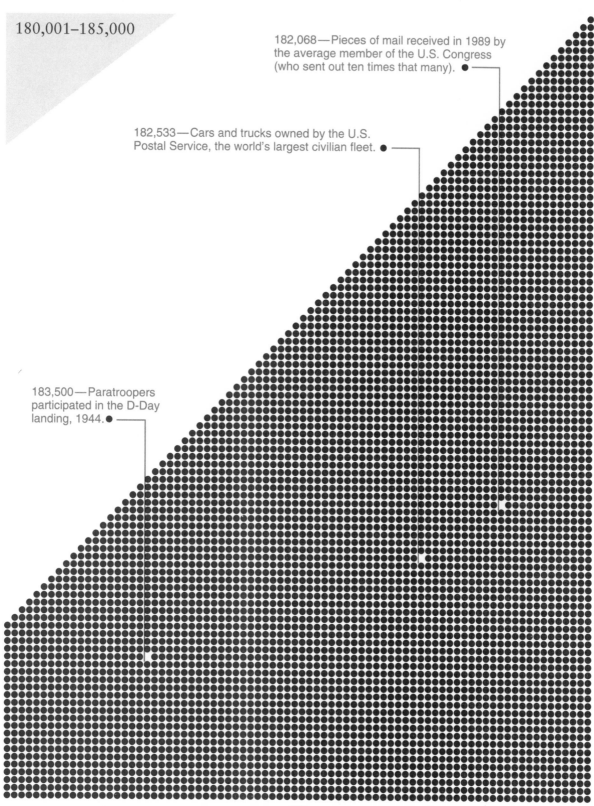

180,001–185,000

182,068—Pieces of mail received in 1989 by the average member of the U.S. Congress (who sent out ten times that many). ●

182,533—Cars and trucks owned by the U.S. Postal Service, the world's largest civilian fleet. ●

183,500—Paratroopers participated in the D-Day landing, 1944. ●

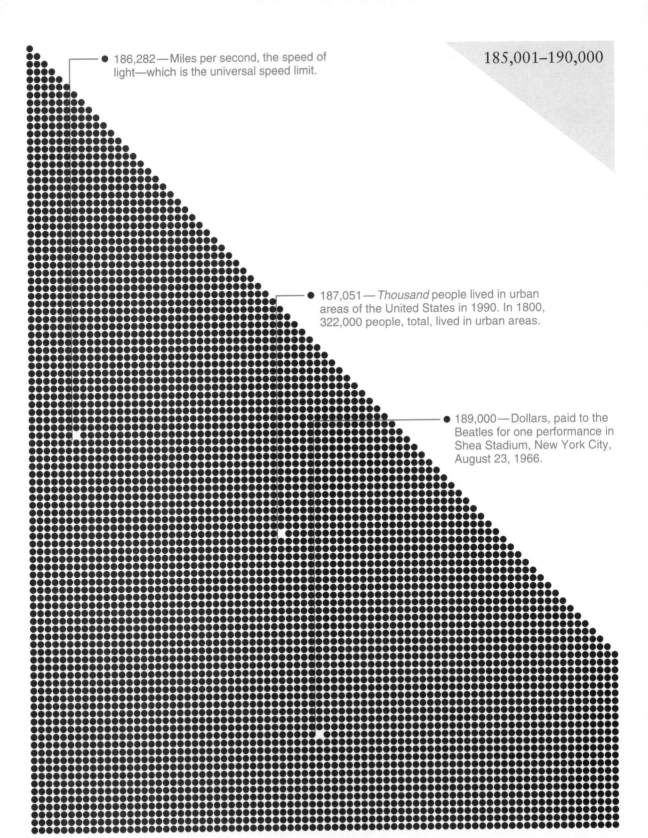

186,282—Miles per second, the speed of light—which is the universal speed limit.

187,051—*Thousand* people lived in urban areas of the United States in 1990. In 1800, 322,000 people, total, lived in urban areas.

189,000—Dollars, paid to the Beatles for one performance in Shea Stadium, New York City, August 23, 1966.

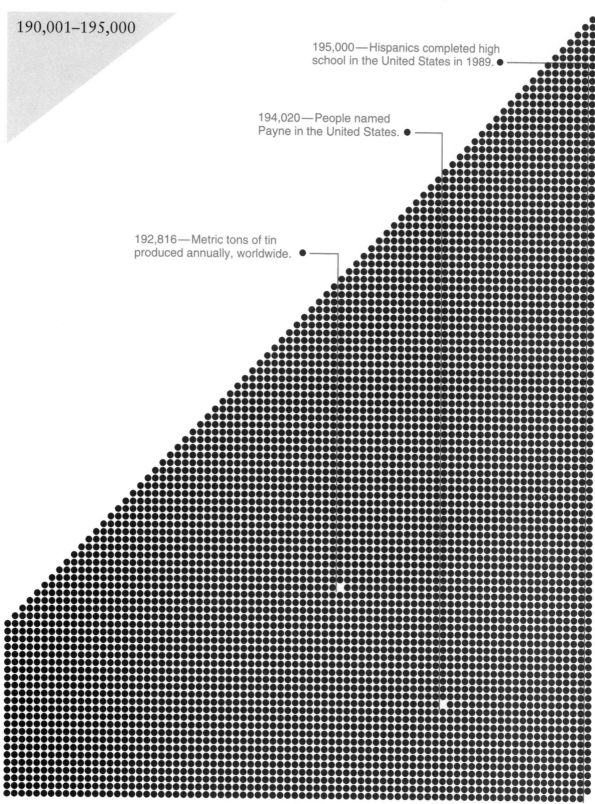

195,000—Hispanics completed high
school in the United States in 1989. ●

194,020—People named
Payne in the United States. ●

192,816—Metric tons of tin
produced annually, worldwide. ●

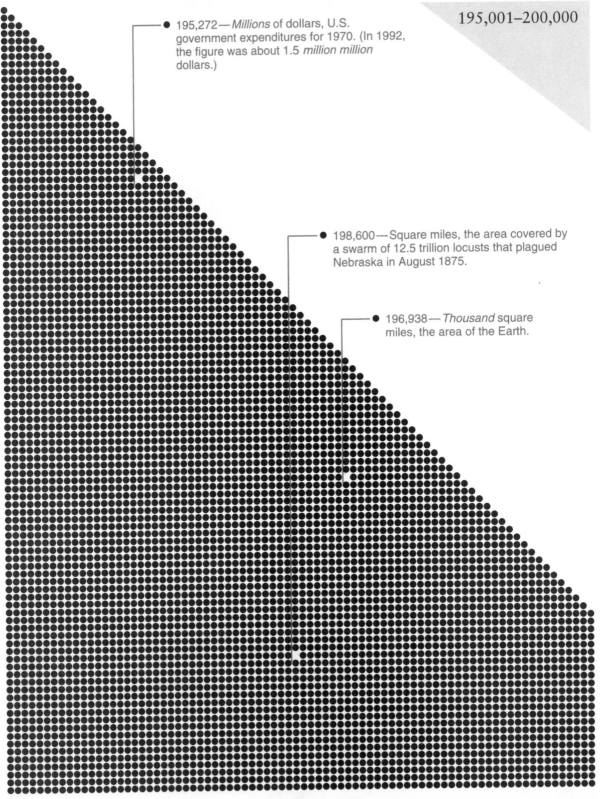

195,272—*Millions* of dollars, U.S. government expenditures for 1970. (In 1992, the figure was about 1.5 *million million* dollars.)

198,600—Square miles, the area covered by a swarm of 12.5 trillion locusts that plagued Nebraska in August 1875.

196,938—*Thousand* square miles, the area of the Earth.

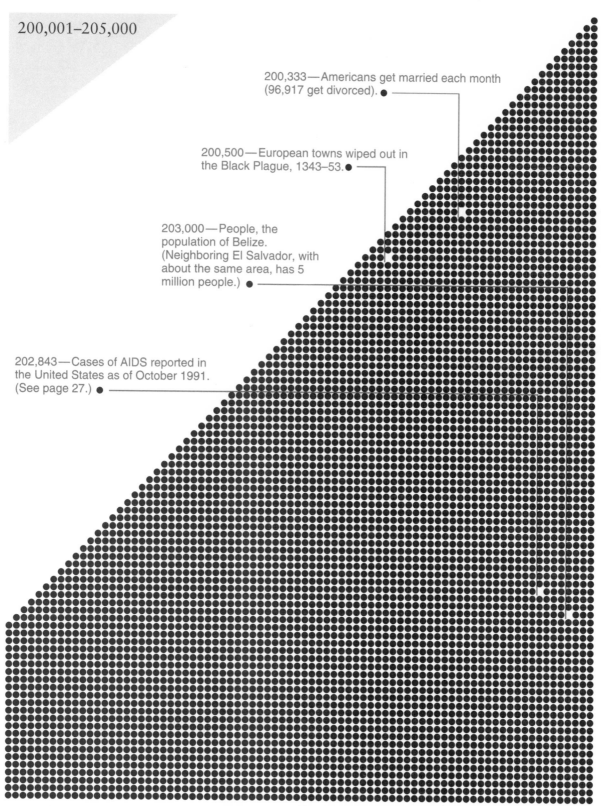

200,333—Americans get married each month
(96,917 get divorced). ●

200,500—European towns wiped out in
the Black Plague, 1343–53. ●

203,000—People, the
population of Belize.
(Neighboring El Salvador, with
about the same area, has 5
million people.) ●

202,843—Cases of AIDS reported in
the United States as of October 1991.
(See page 27.) ●

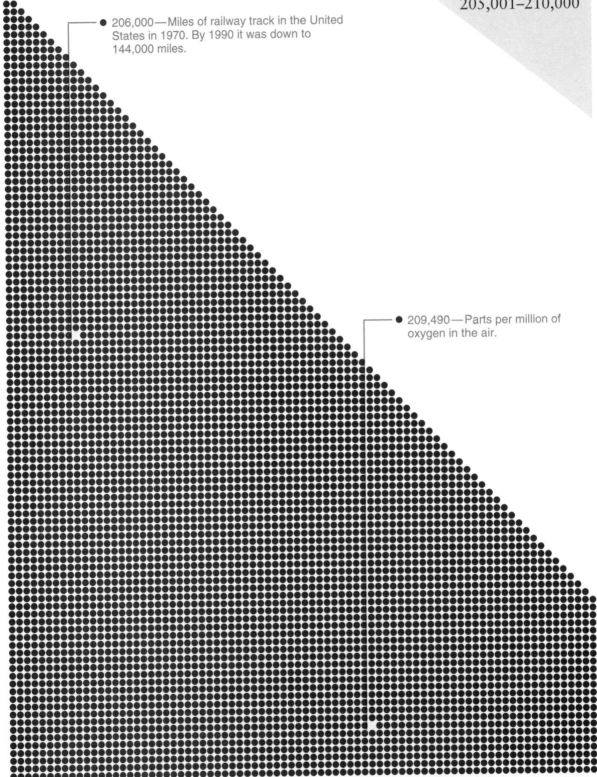

● 206,000—Miles of railway track in the United States in 1970. By 1990 it was down to 144,000 miles.

● 209,490—Parts per million of oxygen in the air.

212,269—Mercury cars cranked out by
the Ford Motor Company in 1991. ●

212,612—Acres of wild and
scenic rivers in the U.S.
National Parks system. ●

214,581—Tons of limestone moved each
year for the thirty years it took four thousand
workers to build the Great Pyramid of
Cheops, ca. 2580 B.C. (Even so, the pyramid
ended up only half the size of the
Quetzalcoatl pyramid outside Mexico City.) ●

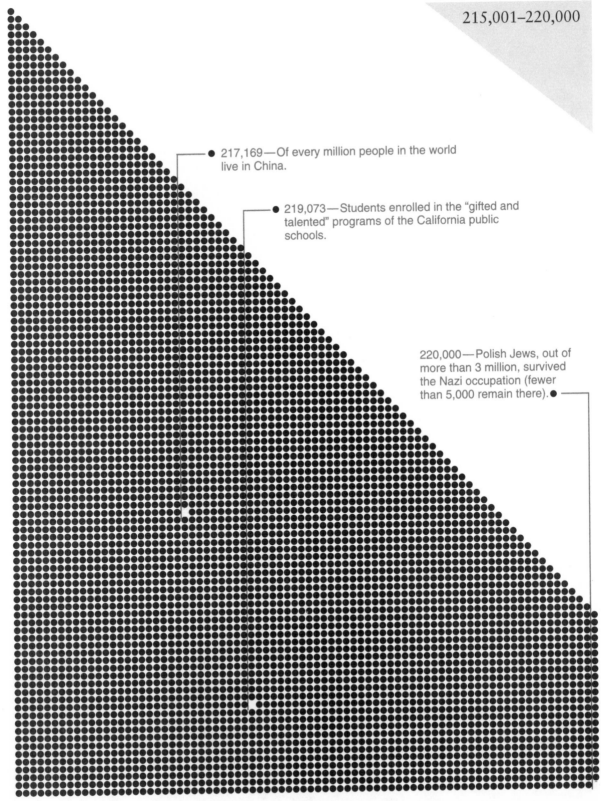

217,169—Of every million people in the world
live in China.

219,073—Students enrolled in the "gifted and
talented" programs of the California public
schools.

220,000—Polish Jews, out of
more than 3 million, survived
the Nazi occupation (fewer
than 5,000 remain there).

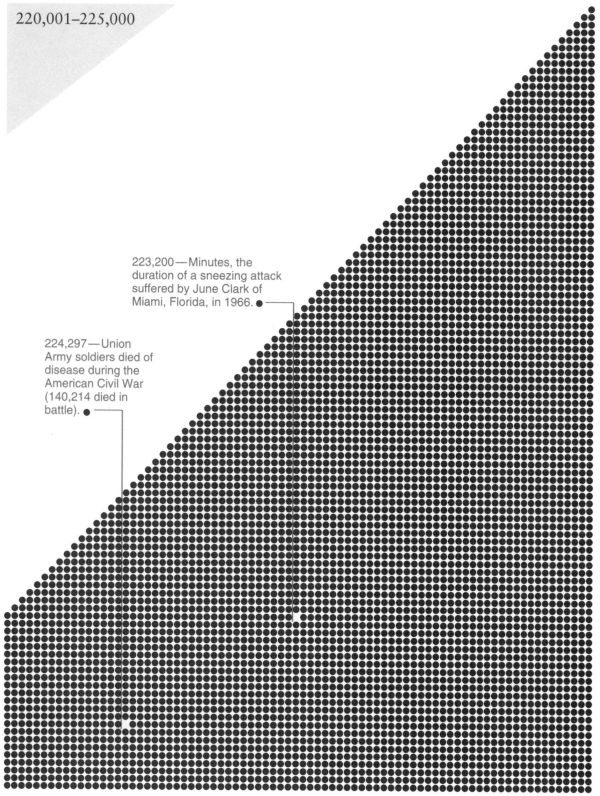

223,200—Minutes, the duration of a sneezing attack suffered by June Clark of Miami, Florida, in 1966. ●—

224,297—Union Army soldiers died of disease during the American Civil War (140,214 died in battle). ●—

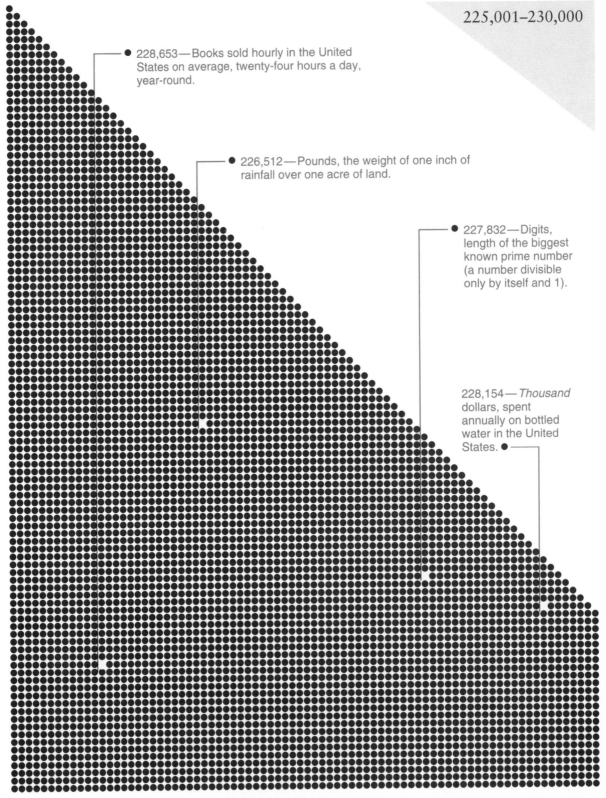

228,653—Books sold hourly in the United States on average, twenty-four hours a day, year-round.

226,512—Pounds, the weight of one inch of rainfall over one acre of land.

227,832—Digits, length of the biggest known prime number (a number divisible only by itself and 1).

228,154—*Thousand* dollars, spent annually on bottled water in the United States.

233,710—Businesses started by Americans in 1987 (50,389 went belly-up). ●

231,472—Daily circulation of the *Hartford Courant,* America's oldest continuously published daily newspaper, in 1993. (Its circulation was 8,000 during the American Revolution.) ●

231,937—Turnstile jumpers in one day on the New York City subway system, just after the 1991 fare increase. ●

232,985—Foreign tourists arrive in the United States every week. ●

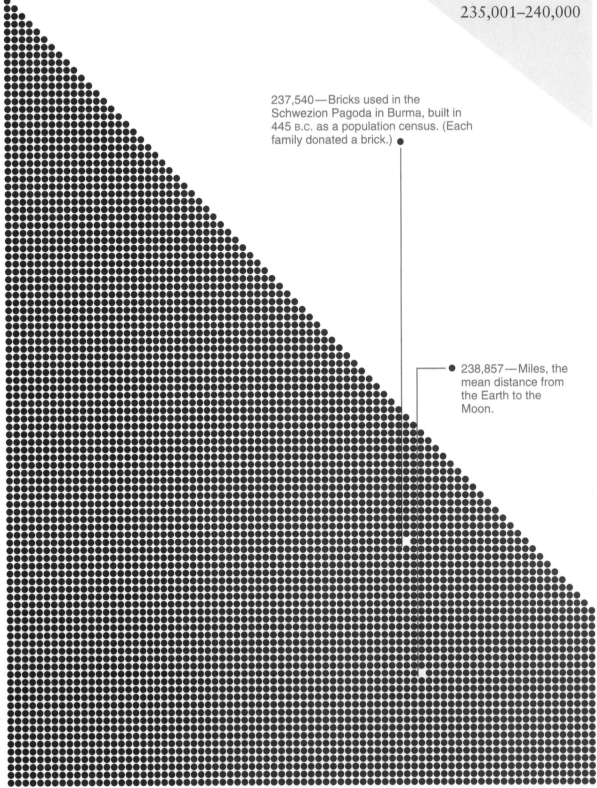

237,540—Bricks used in the Schwezion Pagoda in Burma, built in 445 B.C. as a population census. (Each family donated a brick.)

238,857—Miles, the mean distance from the Earth to the Moon.

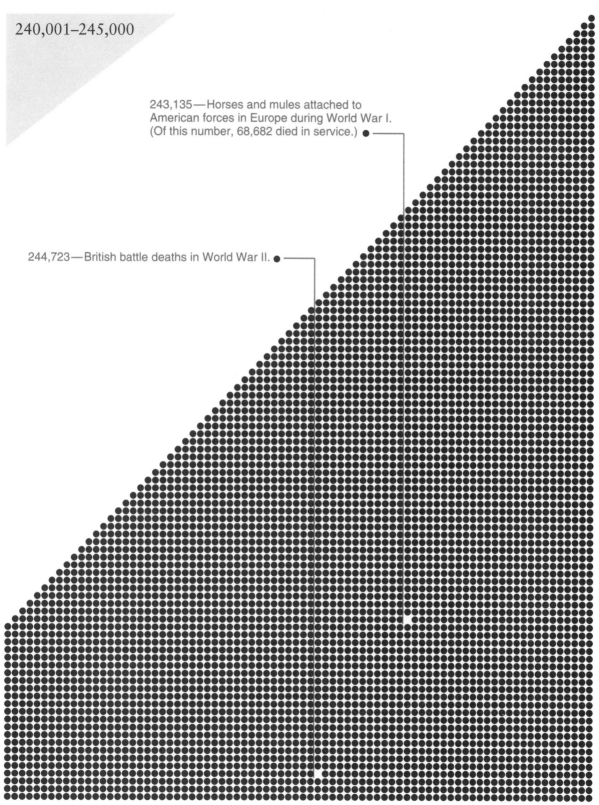

243,135—Horses and mules attached to
American forces in Europe during World War I.
(Of this number, 68,682 died in service.) ●

244,723—British battle deaths in World War II. ●

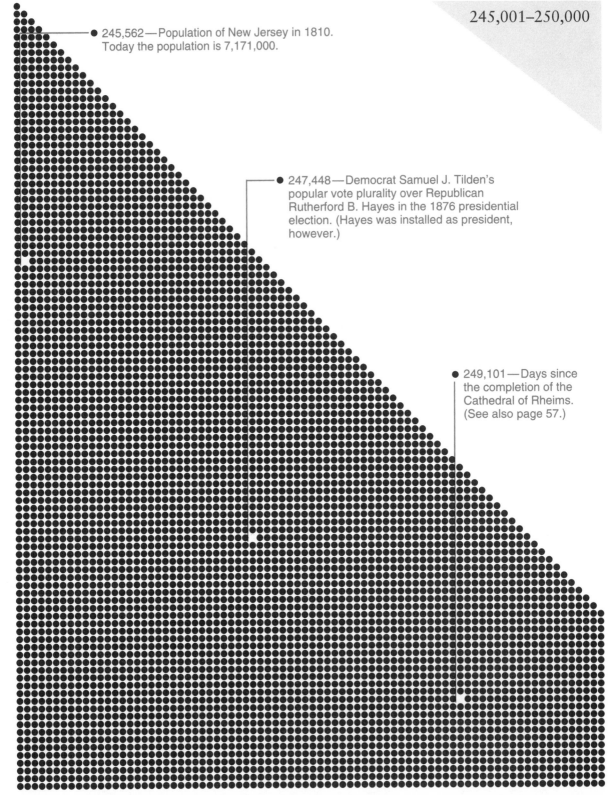

245,562—Population of New Jersey in 1810. Today the population is 7,171,000.

247,448—Democrat Samuel J. Tilden's popular vote plurality over Republican Rutherford B. Hayes in the 1876 presidential election. (Hayes was installed as president, however.)

249,101—Days since the completion of the Cathedral of Rheims. (See also page 57.)

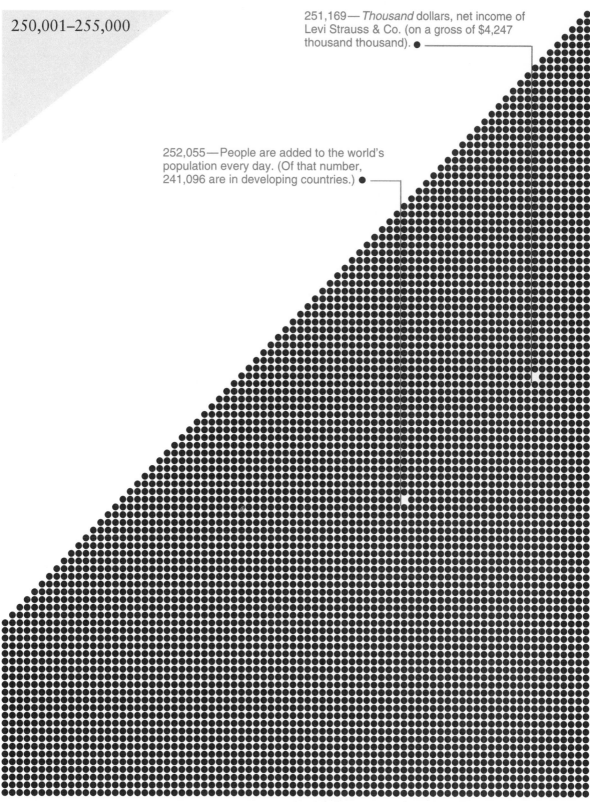

251,169— *Thousand* dollars, net income of Levi Strauss & Co. (on a gross of $4,247 thousand thousand). ●

252,055—People are added to the world's population every day. (Of that number, 241,096 are in developing countries.) ●

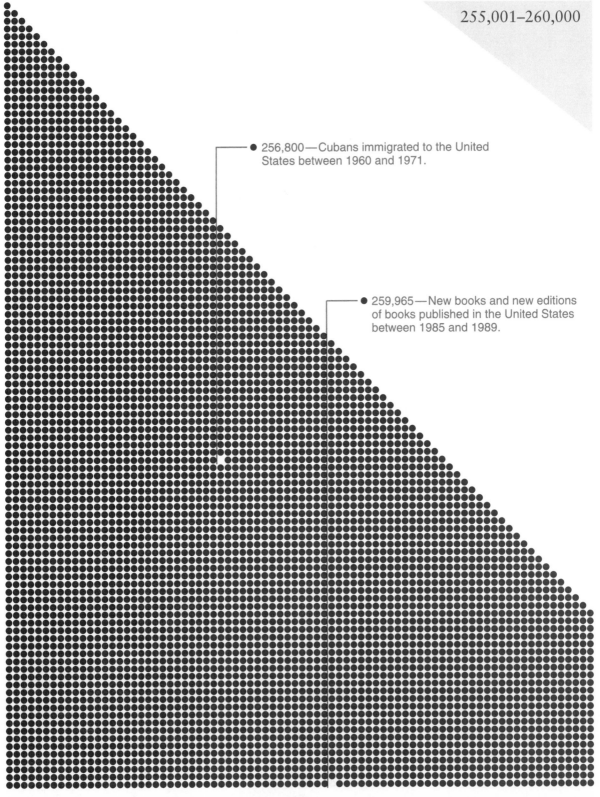

256,800—Cubans immigrated to the United
States between 1960 and 1971.

259,965—New books and new editions
of books published in the United States
between 1985 and 1989.

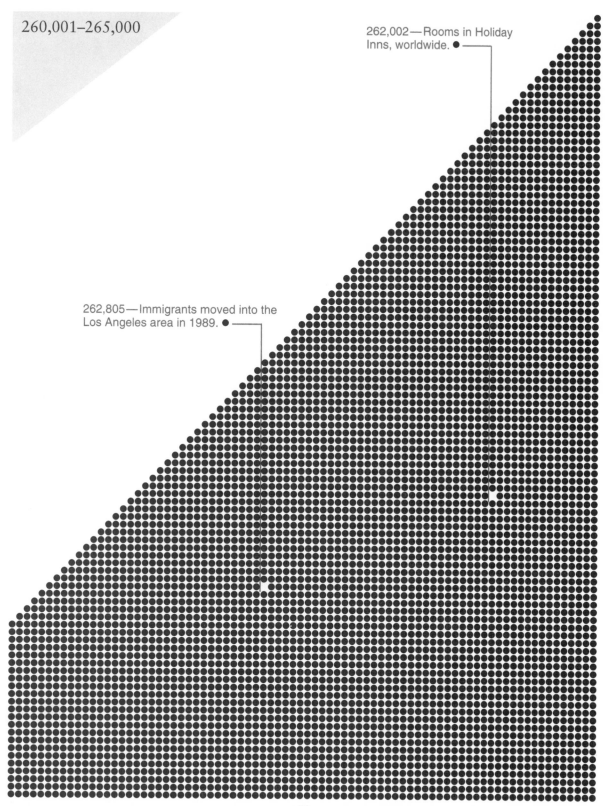

260,001–265,000

262,002—Rooms in Holiday Inns, worldwide. ●

262,805—Immigrants moved into the Los Angeles area in 1989. ●

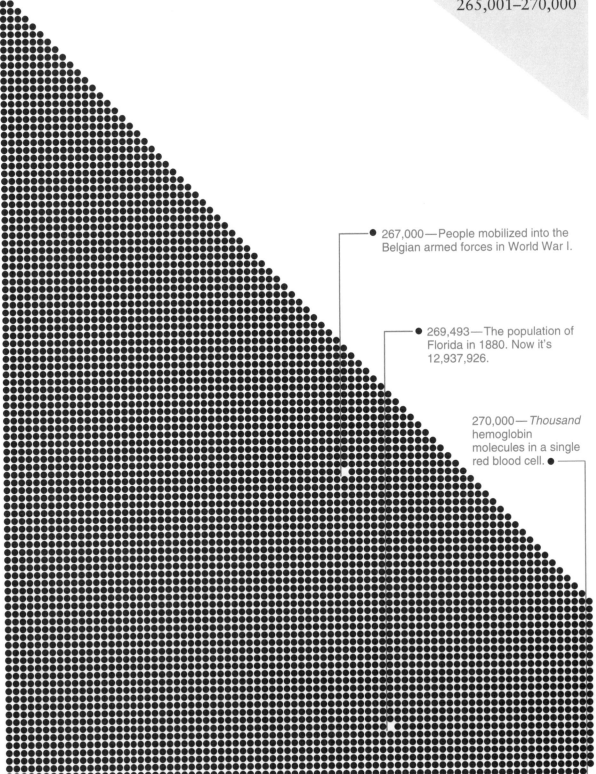

267,000—People mobilized into the Belgian armed forces in World War I.

269,493—The population of Florida in 1880. Now it's 12,937,926.

270,000—*Thousand* hemoglobin molecules in a single red blood cell.

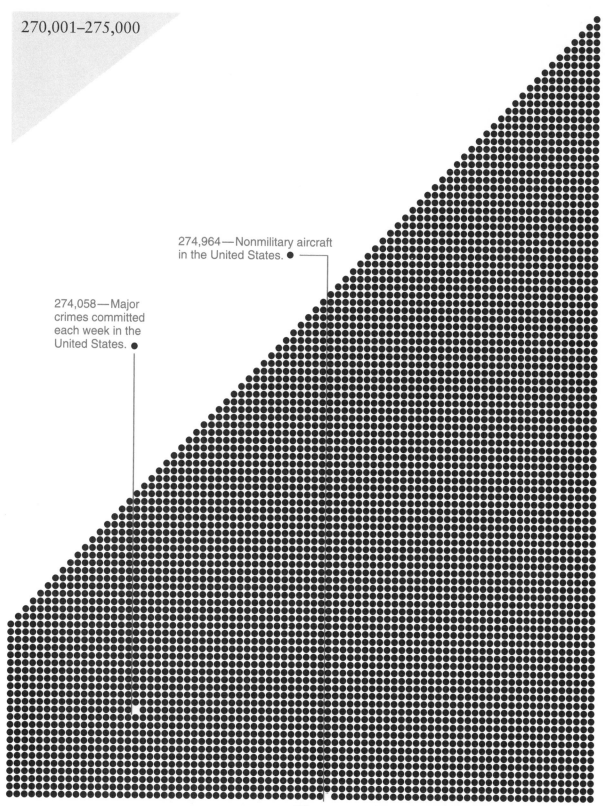

270,001–275,000

274,964—Nonmilitary aircraft in the United States. ●

274,058—Major crimes committed each week in the United States. ●

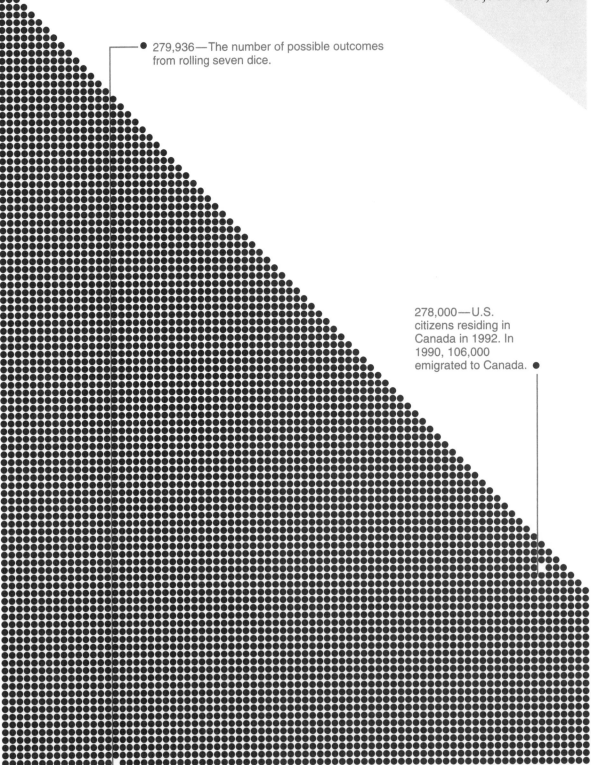

279,936—The number of possible outcomes from rolling seven dice.

278,000—U.S. citizens residing in Canada in 1992. In 1990, 106,000 emigrated to Canada.

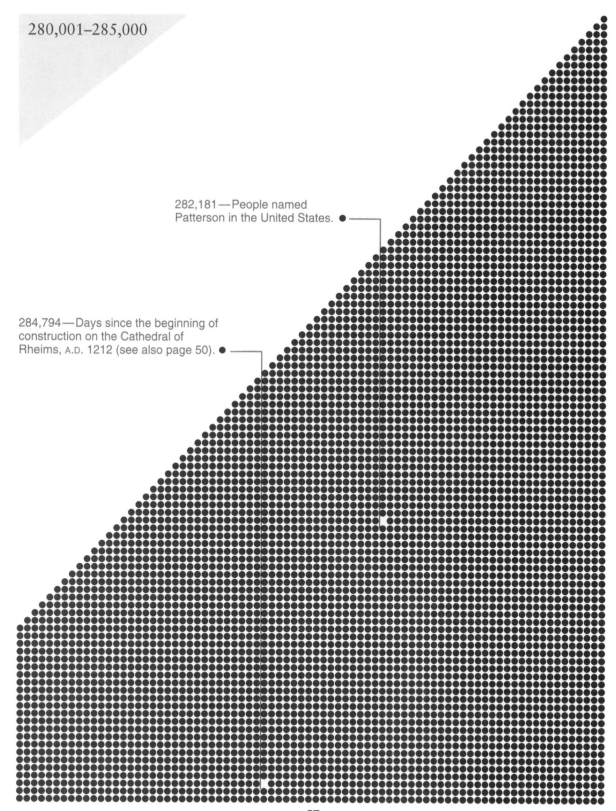

282,181—People named
Patterson in the United States. ●

284,794—Days since the beginning of
construction on the Cathedral of
Rheims, A.D. 1212 (see also page 50). ●

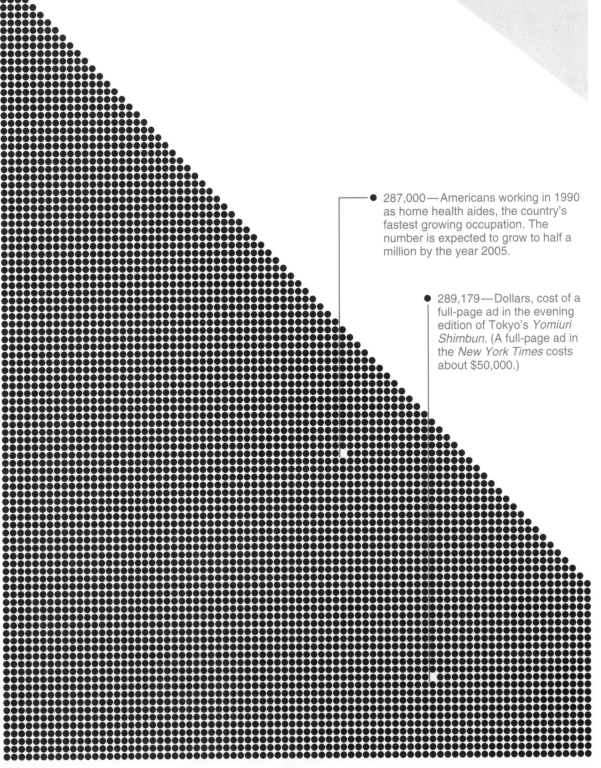

287,000—Americans working in 1990 as home health aides, the country's fastest growing occupation. The number is expected to grow to half a million by the year 2005.

289,179—Dollars, cost of a full-page ad in the evening edition of Tokyo's *Yomiuri Shimbun.* (A full-page ad in the *New York Times* costs about $50,000.)

291,080—Square miles in the five Great Lakes of North America (about the size of Turkey). ●

291,557—Americans killed in World War II. ●

291,446—Americans injure themselves annually with or on chairs, sofas, and sofa beds (1988). ●

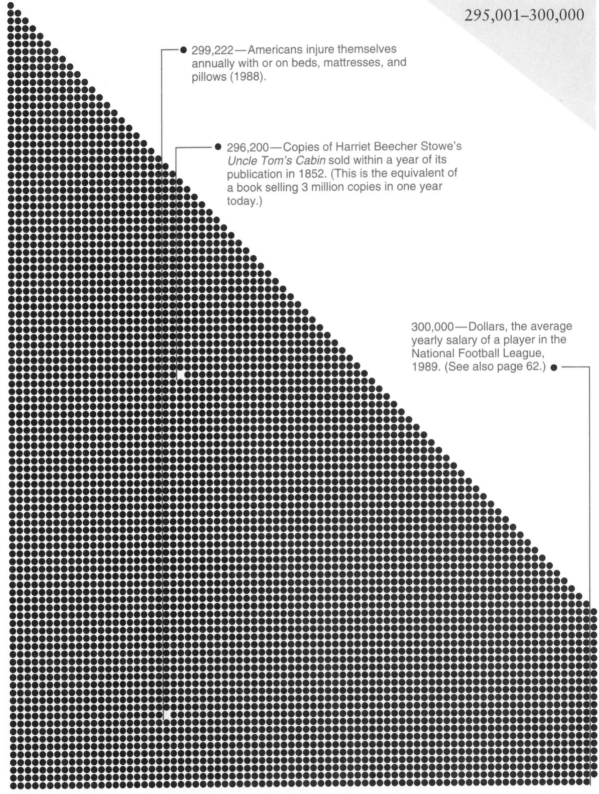

299,222—Americans injure themselves annually with or on beds, mattresses, and pillows (1988).

296,200—Copies of Harriet Beecher Stowe's *Uncle Tom's Cabin* sold within a year of its publication in 1852. (This is the equivalent of a book selling 3 million copies in one year today.)

300,000—Dollars, the average yearly salary of a player in the National Football League, 1989. (See also page 62.)

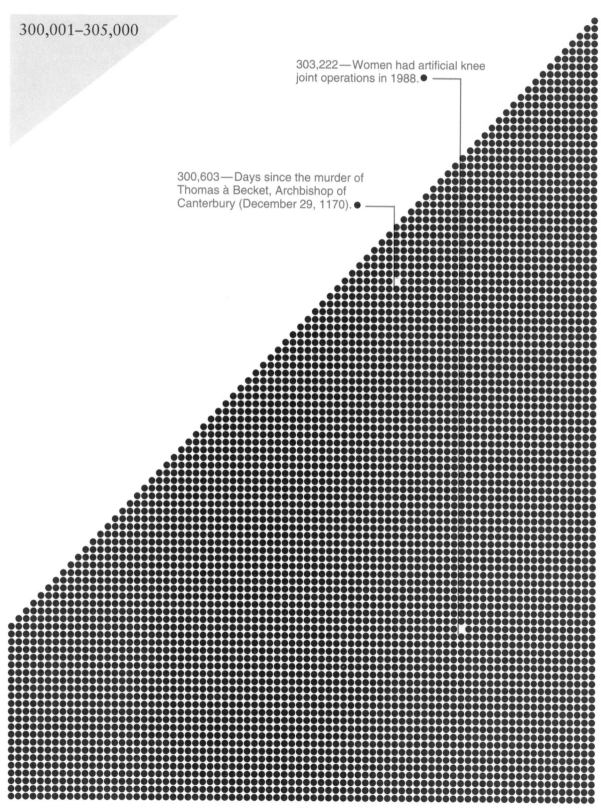

303,222—Women had artificial knee joint operations in 1988.●

300,603—Days since the murder of Thomas à Becket, Archbishop of Canterbury (December 29, 1170). ●

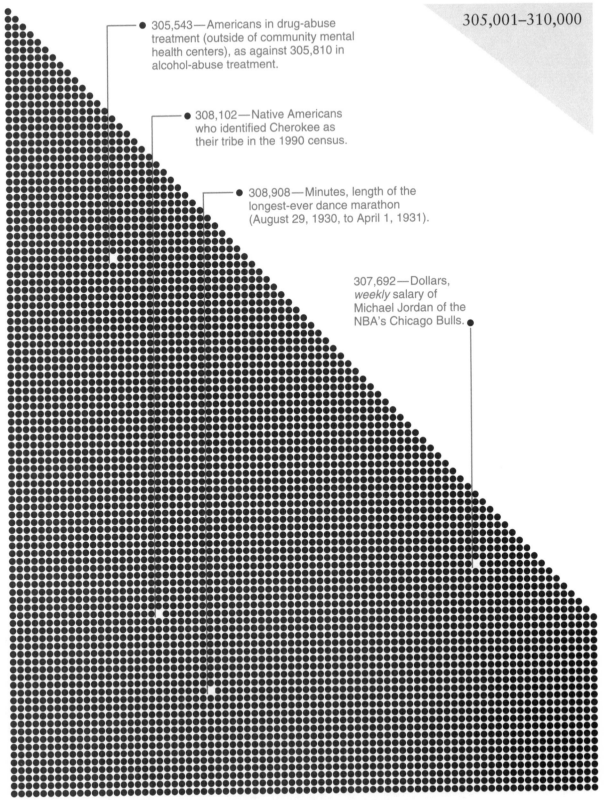

305,543—Americans in drug-abuse treatment (outside of community mental health centers), as against 305,810 in alcohol-abuse treatment.

308,102—Native Americans who identified Cherokee as their tribe in the 1990 census.

308,908—Minutes, length of the longest-ever dance marathon (August 29, 1930, to April 1, 1931).

307,692—Dollars, *weekly* salary of Michael Jordan of the NBA's Chicago Bulls.

311,111—Cokes are quaffed per minute around the world. ●

311,178—People, on average, have signed up for the Discovery cable TV channel every two weeks since 1985. (See also pages 65 and 79.)●

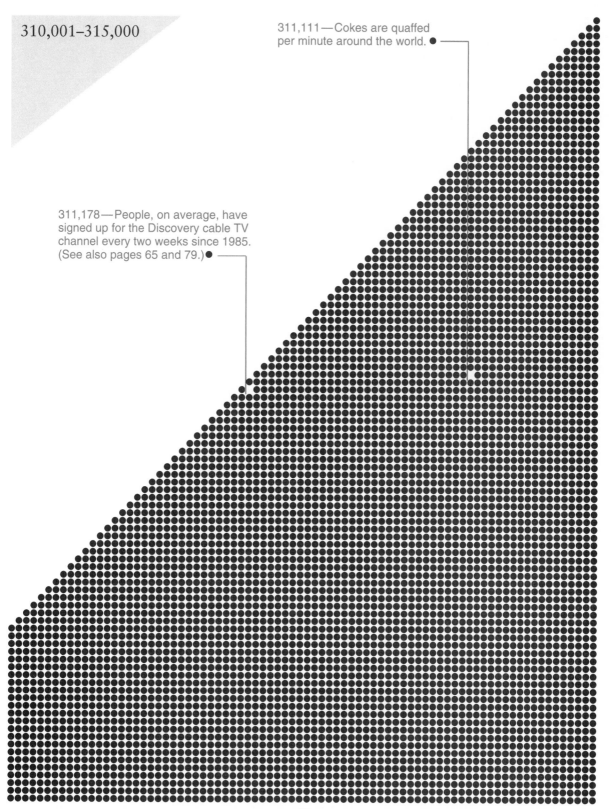

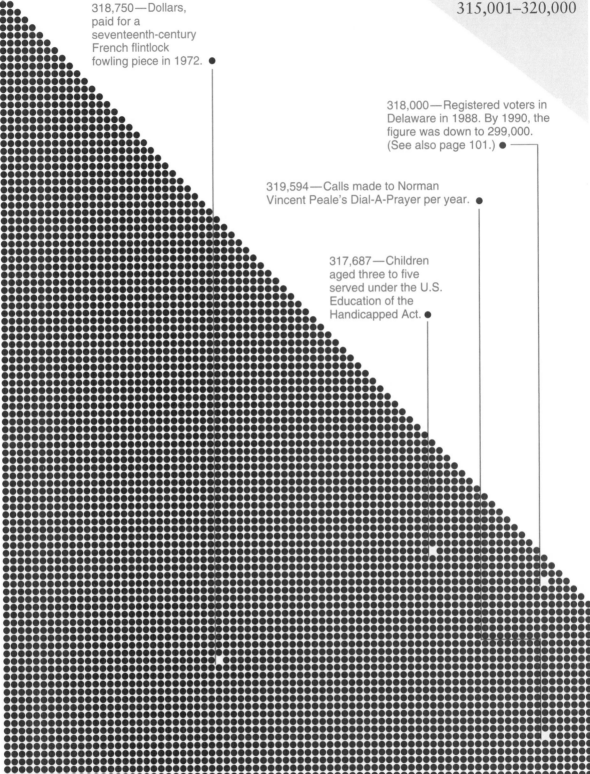

318,750—Dollars,
paid for a
seventeenth-century
French flintlock
fowling piece in 1972. ●

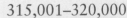

318,000—Registered voters in
Delaware in 1988. By 1990, the
figure was down to 299,000.
(See also page 101.) ●

319,594—Calls made to Norman
Vincent Peale's Dial-A-Prayer per year. ●

317,687—Children
aged three to five
served under the U.S.
Education of the
Handicapped Act. ●

321,178—Households, on average, have been signing up to get MTV every three weeks since August 1981. ●

324,870—The U.S. patent issued to D. J. Kennedy in 1929 for his epoch-making invention: the padded bra. ●

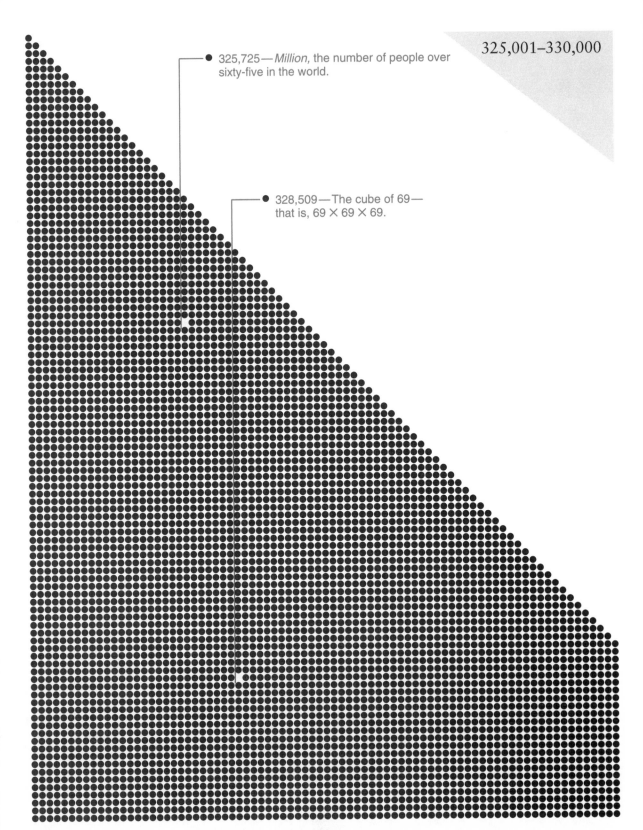

325,725—*Million,* the number of people over sixty-five in the world.

328,509—The cube of 69—that is, 69 × 69 × 69.

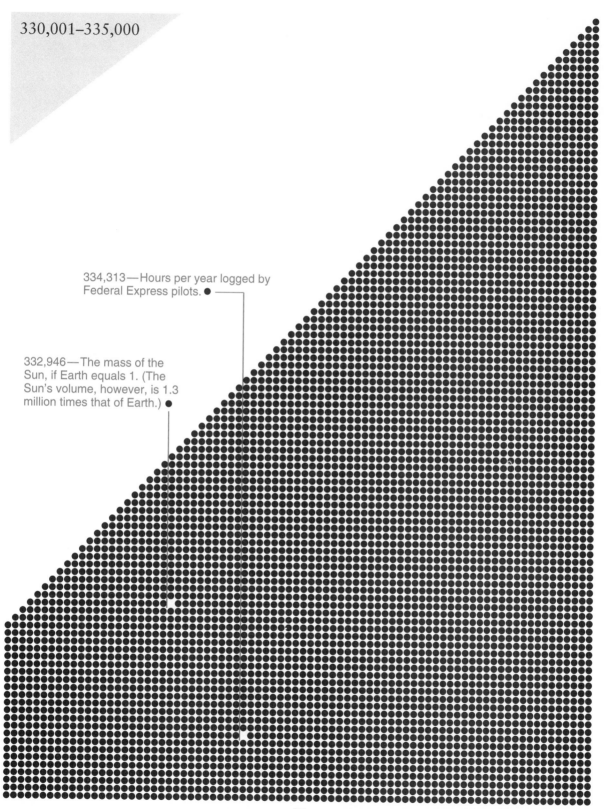

334,313—Hours per year logged by
Federal Express pilots. ●

332,946—The mass of the
Sun, if Earth equals 1. (The
Sun's volume, however, is 1.3
million times that of Earth.) ●

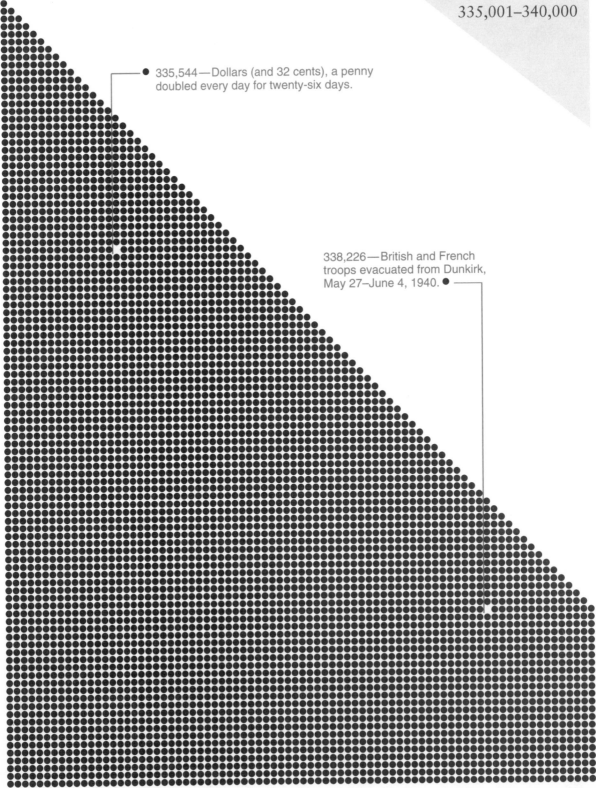

335,544—Dollars (and 32 cents), a penny doubled every day for twenty-six days.

338,226—British and French troops evacuated from Dunkirk, May 27–June 4, 1940.

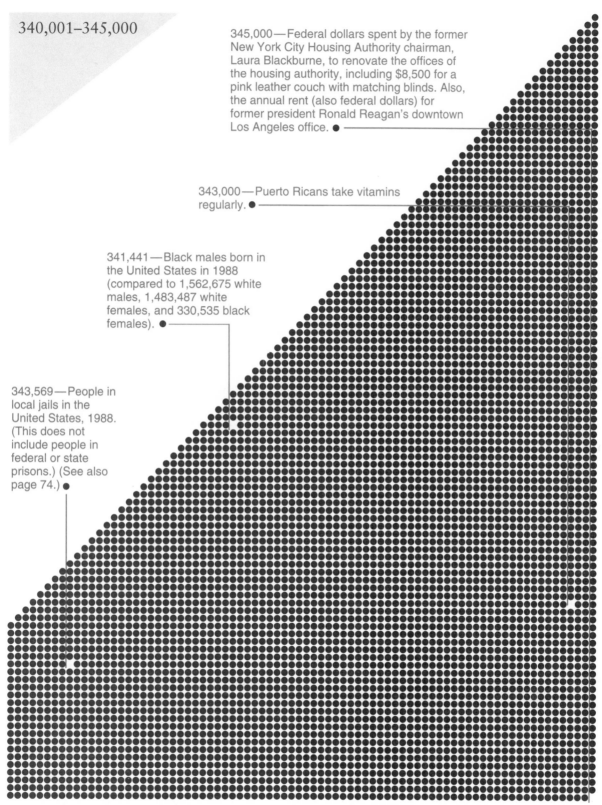

345,000—Federal dollars spent by the former New York City Housing Authority chairman, Laura Blackburne, to renovate the offices of the housing authority, including $8,500 for a pink leather couch with matching blinds. Also, the annual rent (also federal dollars) for former president Ronald Reagan's downtown Los Angeles office. ●

343,000—Puerto Ricans take vitamins regularly. ●

341,441—Black males born in the United States in 1988 (compared to 1,562,675 white males, 1,483,487 white females, and 330,535 black females). ●

343,569—People in local jails in the United States, 1988. (This does not include people in federal or state prisons.) (See also page 74.) ●

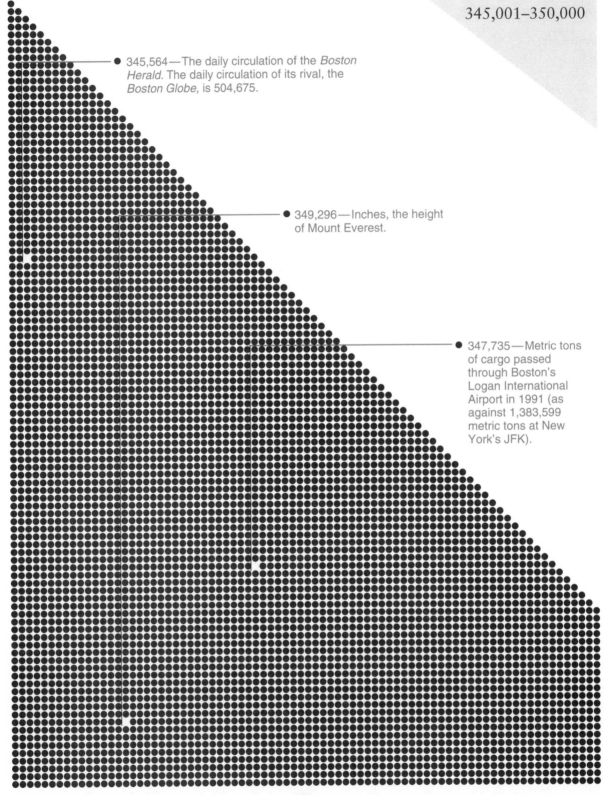

● 345,564—The daily circulation of the *Boston Herald*. The daily circulation of its rival, the *Boston Globe,* is 504,675.

● 349,296—Inches, the height of Mount Everest.

● 347,735—Metric tons of cargo passed through Boston's Logan International Airport in 1991 (as against 1,383,599 metric tons at New York's JFK).

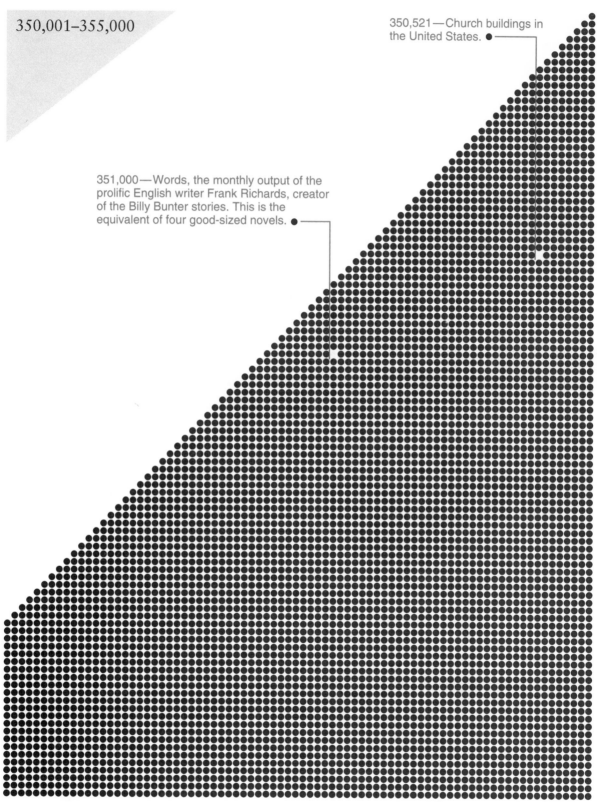

350,521—Church buildings in the United States. ●

351,000—Words, the monthly output of the prolific English writer Frank Richards, creator of the Billy Bunter stories. This is the equivalent of four good-sized novels. ●

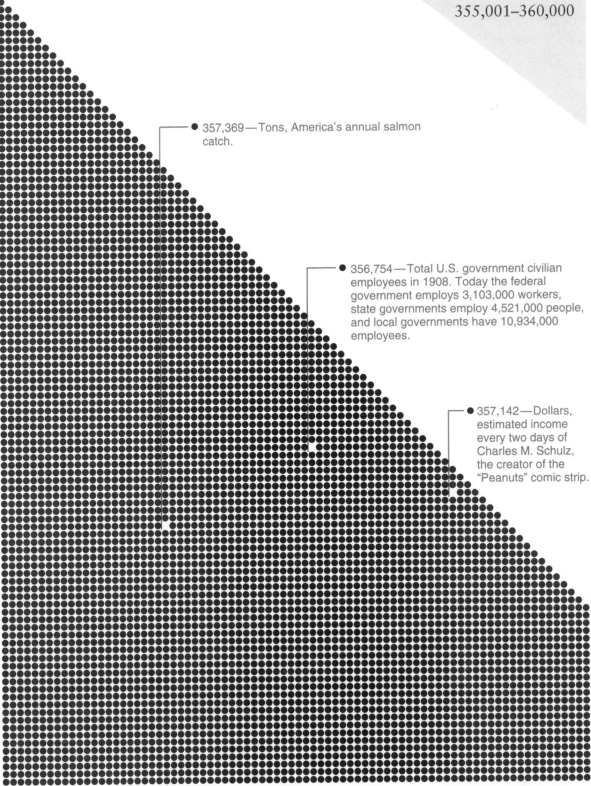

357,369—Tons, America's annual salmon catch.

356,754—Total U.S. government civilian employees in 1908. Today the federal government employs 3,103,000 workers, state governments employ 4,521,000 people, and local governments have 10,934,000 employees.

357,142—Dollars, estimated income every two days of Charles M. Schulz, the creator of the "Peanuts" comic strip.

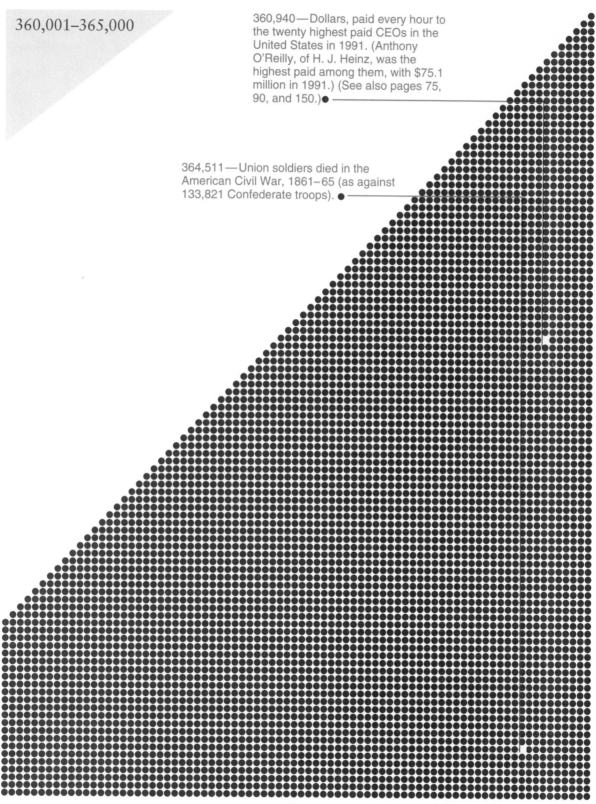

360,940—Dollars, paid every hour to the twenty highest paid CEOs in the United States in 1991. (Anthony O'Reilly, of H. J. Heinz, was the highest paid among them, with $75.1 million in 1991.) (See also pages 75, 90, and 150.)●

364,511—Union soldiers died in the American Civil War, 1861–65 (as against 133,821 Confederate troops). ●

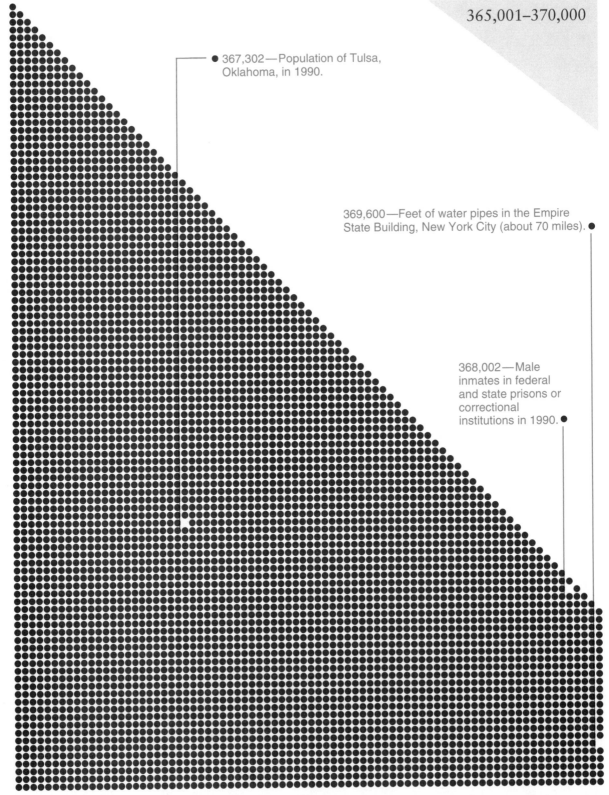

367,302—Population of Tulsa, Oklahoma, in 1990.

369,600—Feet of water pipes in the Empire State Building, New York City (about 70 miles).

368,002—Male inmates in federal and state prisons or correctional institutions in 1990.

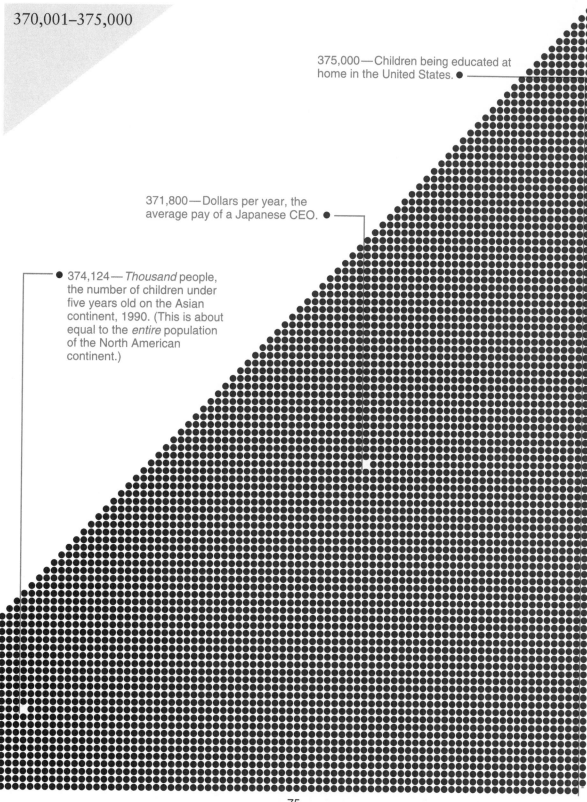

375,000—Children being educated at
home in the United States. ●

371,800—Dollars per year, the
average pay of a Japanese CEO. ●

● 374,124—*Thousand* people,
the number of children under
five years old on the Asian
continent, 1990. (This is about
equal to the *entire* population
of the North American
continent.)

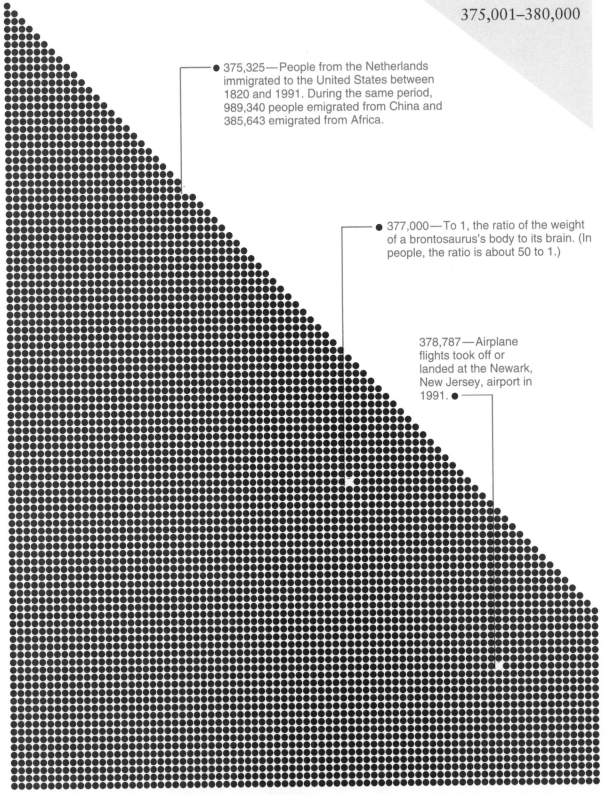

375,325—People from the Netherlands immigrated to the United States between 1820 and 1991. During the same period, 989,340 people emigrated from China and 385,643 emigrated from Africa.

377,000—To 1, the ratio of the weight of a brontosaurus's body to its brain. (In people, the ratio is about 50 to 1.)

378,787—Airplane flights took off or landed at the Newark, New Jersey, airport in 1991.

381,645—Maps in the collection of the
New York Public Library. ●

380,232—Police officers assaulted in the
United States in 1989. By 1991, the number
had shot up to 412,314. ●

383,934—Pieces of sheet music in the
same collection, which also contains
6,511,005 bound volumes. ●

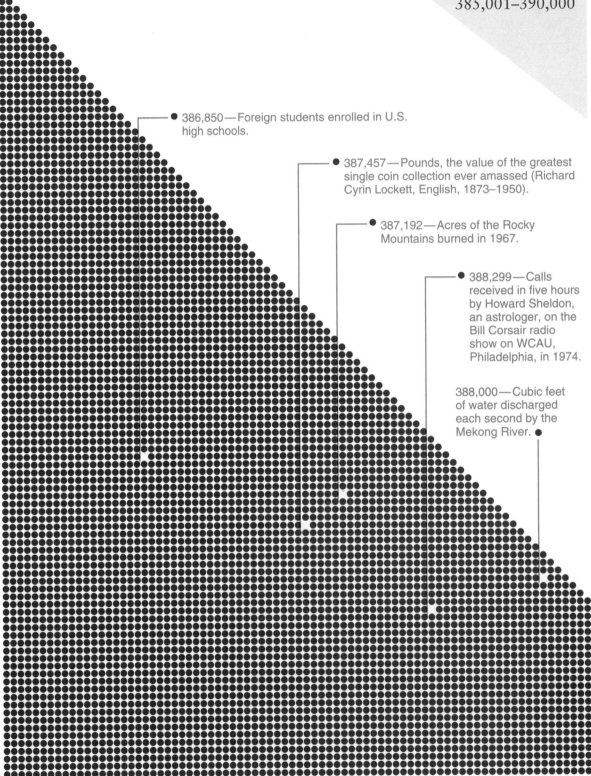

386,850—Foreign students enrolled in U.S. high schools.

387,457—Pounds, the value of the greatest single coin collection ever amassed (Richard Cyrin Lockett, English, 1873–1950).

387,192—Acres of the Rocky Mountains burned in 1967.

388,299—Calls received in five hours by Howard Sheldon, an astrologer, on the Bill Corsair radio show on WCAU, Philadelphia, in 1974.

388,000—Cubic feet of water discharged each second by the Mekong River.

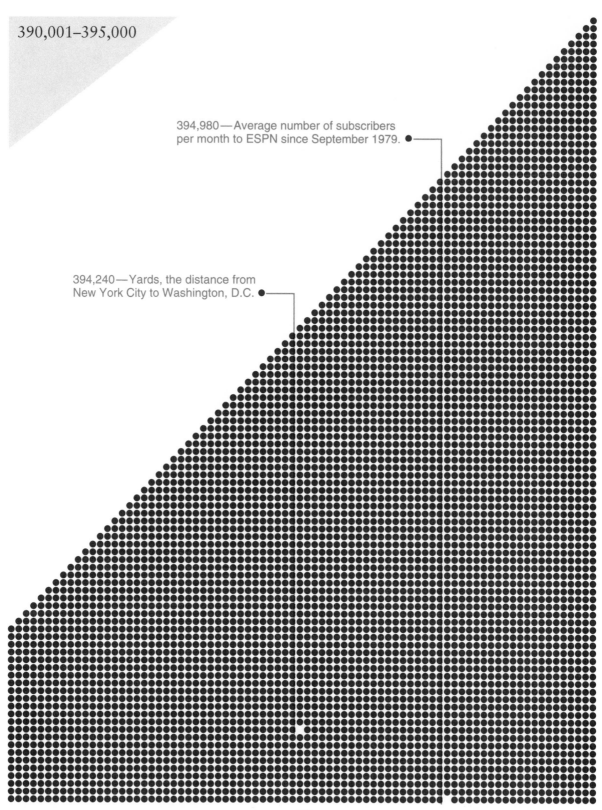

394,980—Average number of subscribers per month to ESPN since September 1979.

394,240—Yards, the distance from New York City to Washington, D.C.

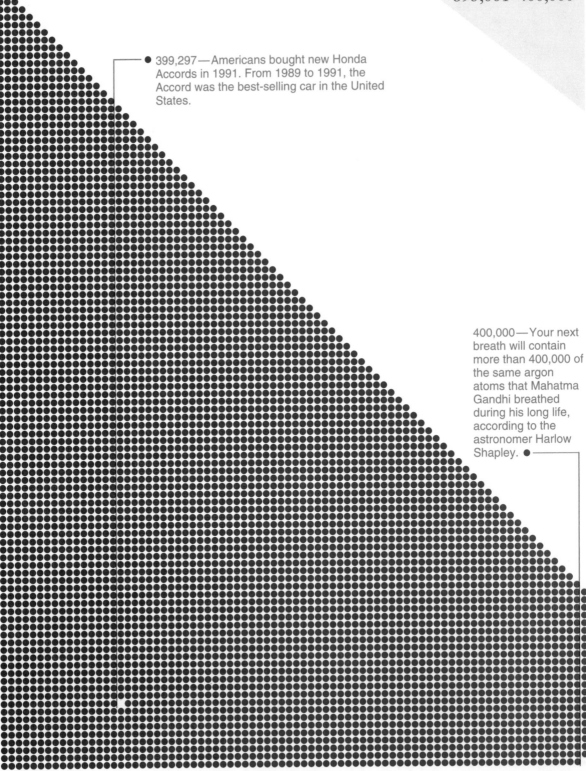

● 399,297—Americans bought new Honda Accords in 1991. From 1989 to 1991, the Accord was the best-selling car in the United States.

400,000—Your next breath will contain more than 400,000 of the same argon atoms that Mahatma Gandhi breathed during his long life, according to the astronomer Harlow Shapley. ●

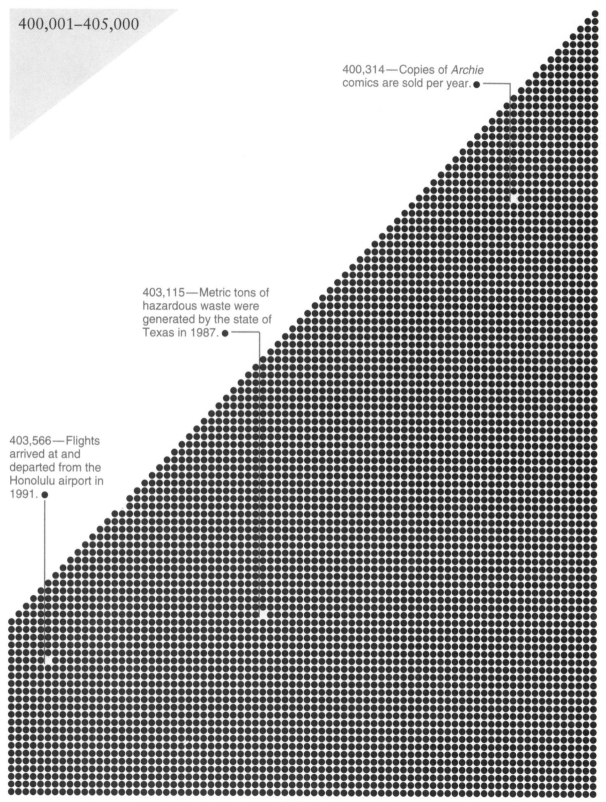

400,001–405,000

400,314—Copies of *Archie* comics are sold per year. ●

403,115—Metric tons of hazardous waste were generated by the state of Texas in 1987. ●

403,566—Flights arrived at and departed from the Honolulu airport in 1991. ●

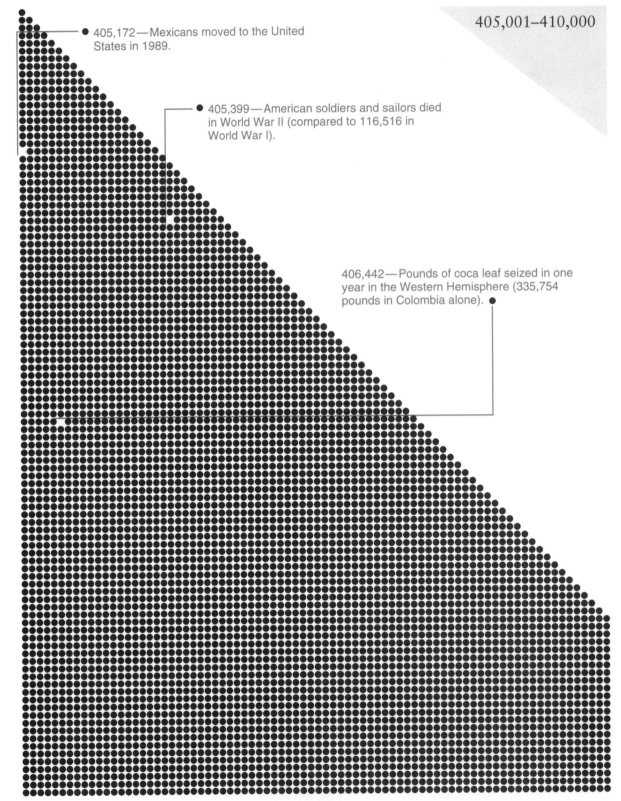

405,172—Mexicans moved to the United States in 1989.

405,399—American soldiers and sailors died in World War II (compared to 116,516 in World War I).

406,442—Pounds of coca leaf seized in one year in the Western Hemisphere (335,754 pounds in Colombia alone).

415,000—Dollars, the value of the estate of
Dr. William Grier of San Diego, California,
which he left to his two cats in June 1963. ●

414,000—Peak strength of the Greek
army in World War II. ●

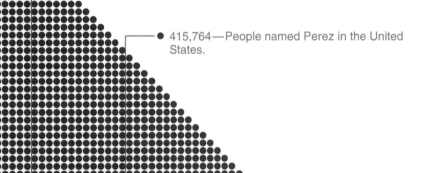

418,403—AIDS cases reported worldwide as of October 1991. The real number is believed to be many times higher.

416,000—Average number of letters received by a first lady during her husband's four-year term (in the pre-Hillary era).

415,764—People named Perez in the United States.

418,692—Dollars, net worth of Bill and Hillary Clinton in 1989. (By 1991 it was up to $700,000.)

424,165—Black-owned firms in the United States in 1987, up from 308,260 in 1982.

420,781—Americans graduated from college with degrees in psychology during the last ten years.

424,302—People of Hispanic origin in Colorado, 1990 (as against 3,661 in Vermont).

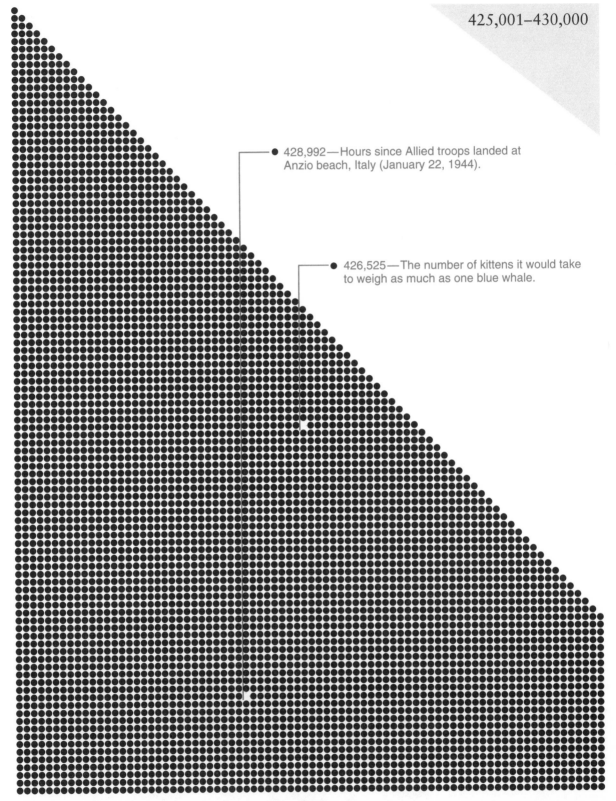

428,992—Hours since Allied troops landed at Anzio beach, Italy (January 22, 1944).

426,525—The number of kittens it would take to weigh as much as one blue whale.

434,038—Dollars, Saudi Arabia's annual military spending per soldier. (The comparable figures are $105,638 for the United States, $21,807 for Iraq, and $3,917 for Turkey.) ●

433,940—Million metric tons of vegetables produced worldwide, annually. ●

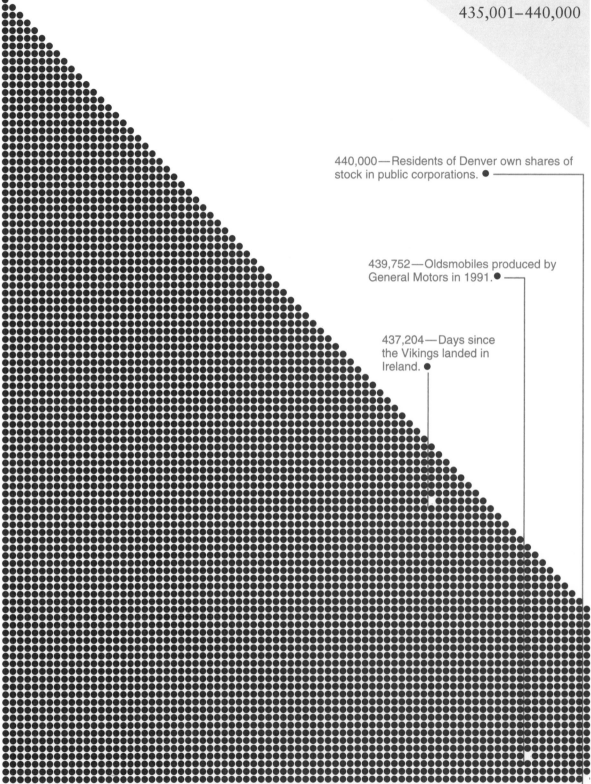

435,001–440,000

440,000—Residents of Denver own shares of stock in public corporations. ●

439,752—Oldsmobiles produced by General Motors in 1991. ●

437,204—Days since the Vikings landed in Ireland. ●

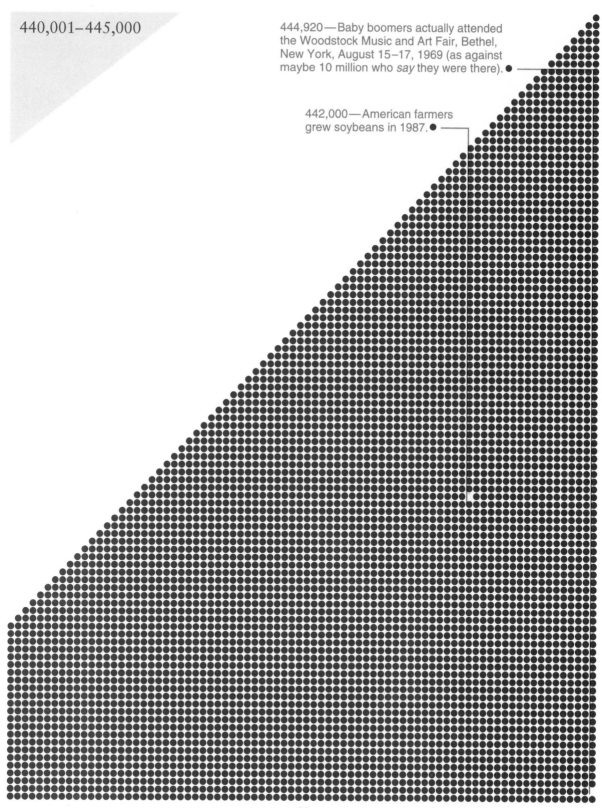

444,920—Baby boomers actually attended the Woodstock Music and Art Fair, Bethel, New York, August 15–17, 1969 (as against maybe 10 million who *say* they were there). ●

442,000—American farmers grew soybeans in 1987. ●

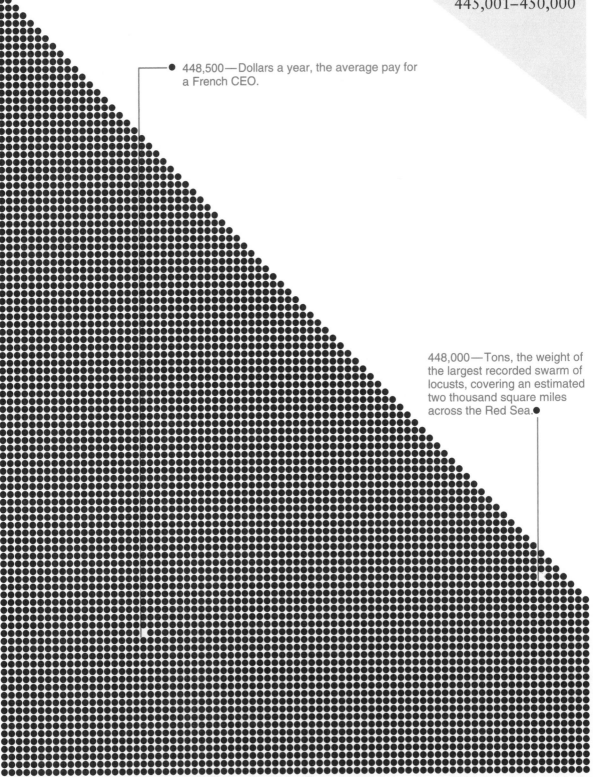

448,500—Dollars a year, the average pay for a French CEO.

448,000—Tons, the weight of the largest recorded swarm of locusts, covering an estimated two thousand square miles across the Red Sea.

452,992—Students enrolled in Roman
Catholic high schools in the United States (as
against 36 in Russian Orthodox high schools). ●

451,000—Dollars, paid by Bruce McNall,
owner of the Los Angeles Kings hockey team,
and Wayne Gretzky for a baseball card in
1991. ●

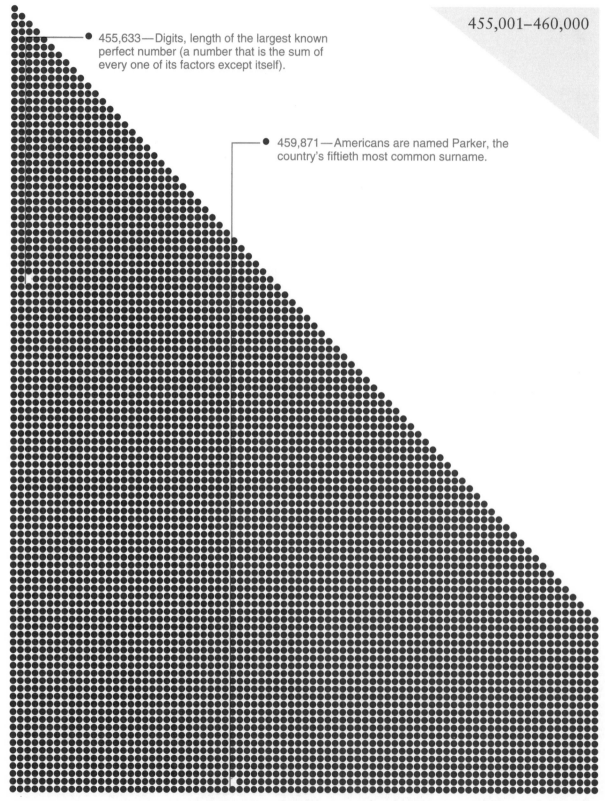

455,633—Digits, length of the largest known perfect number (a number that is the sum of every one of its factors except itself).

459,871—Americans are named Parker, the country's fiftieth most common surname.

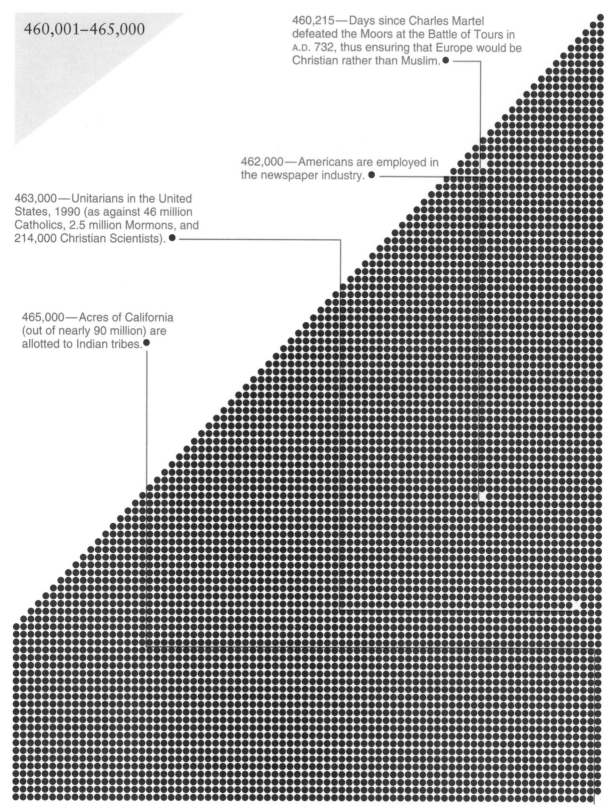

460,001–465,000

460,215—Days since Charles Martel defeated the Moors at the Battle of Tours in A.D. 732, thus ensuring that Europe would be Christian rather than Muslim. ●

462,000—Americans are employed in the newspaper industry. ●

463,000—Unitarians in the United States, 1990 (as against 46 million Catholics, 2.5 million Mormons, and 214,000 Christian Scientists). ●

465,000—Acres of California (out of nearly 90 million) are allotted to Indian tribes.●

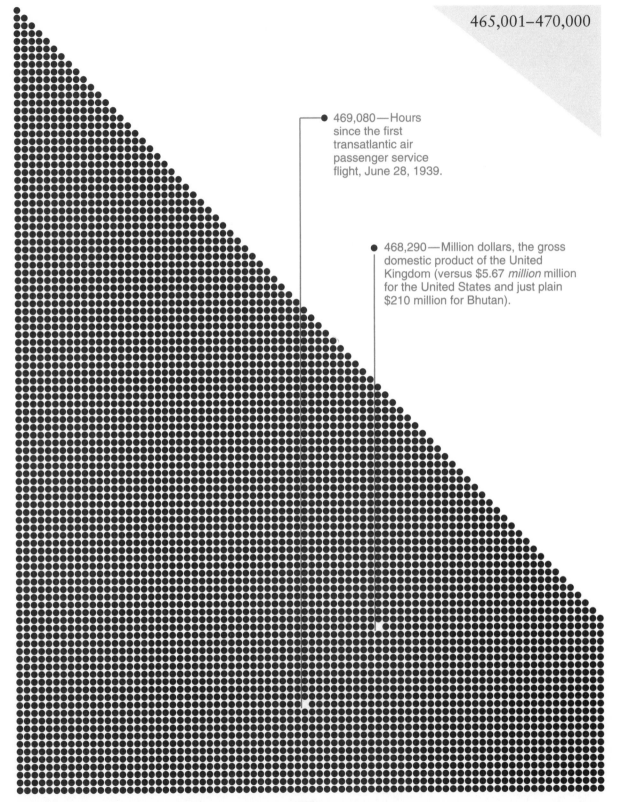

469,080—Hours since the first transatlantic air passenger service flight, June 28, 1939.

468,290—Million dollars, the gross domestic product of the United Kingdom (versus $5.67 *million* million for the United States and just plain $210 million for Bhutan).

470,318—Thousand metric tons of corn produced annually, worldwide.●

471,445—Square miles, the area of South Africa (about the size of Texas, California, and New York State combined).●

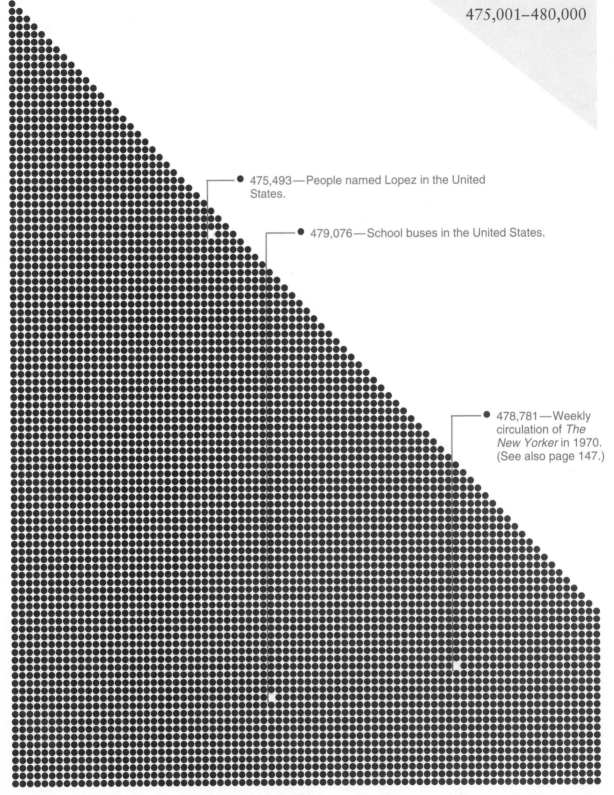

475,493—People named Lopez in the United States.

479,076—School buses in the United States.

478,781—Weekly circulation of *The New Yorker* in 1970. (See also page 147.)

483,000—Riders daily on the buses and
trains of the Washington, D.C., transit system. ●

484,500—Miles, distance by which the
asteroid Hermes missed the Earth on October
30, 1937. ●

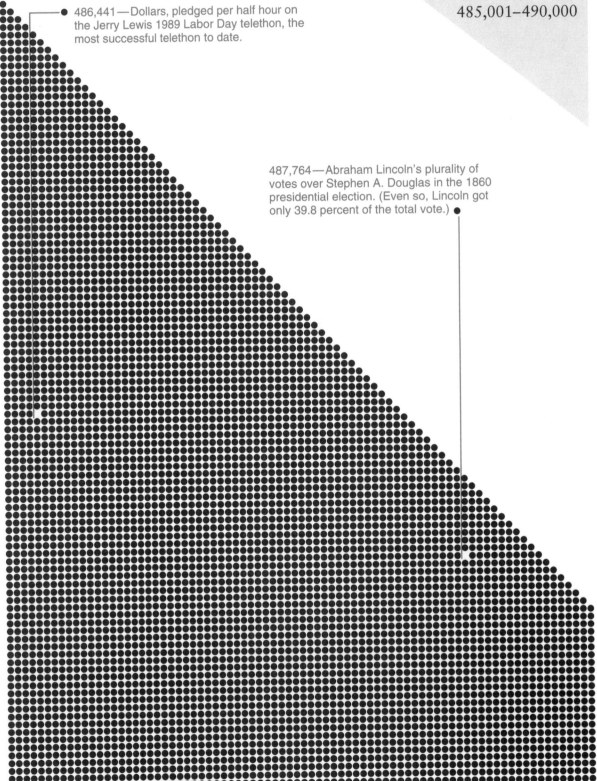

486,441—Dollars, pledged per half hour on the Jerry Lewis 1989 Labor Day telethon, the most successful telethon to date.

487,764—Abraham Lincoln's plurality of votes over Stephen A. Douglas in the 1860 presidential election. (Even so, Lincoln got only 39.8 percent of the total vote.)

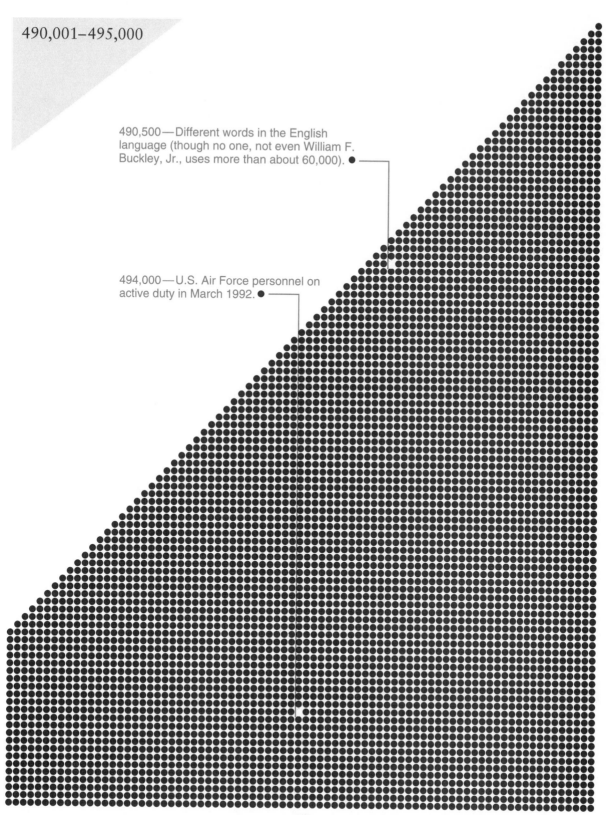

490,500—Different words in the English language (though no one, not even William F. Buckley, Jr., uses more than about 60,000). ●

494,000—U.S. Air Force personnel on active duty in March 1992. ●

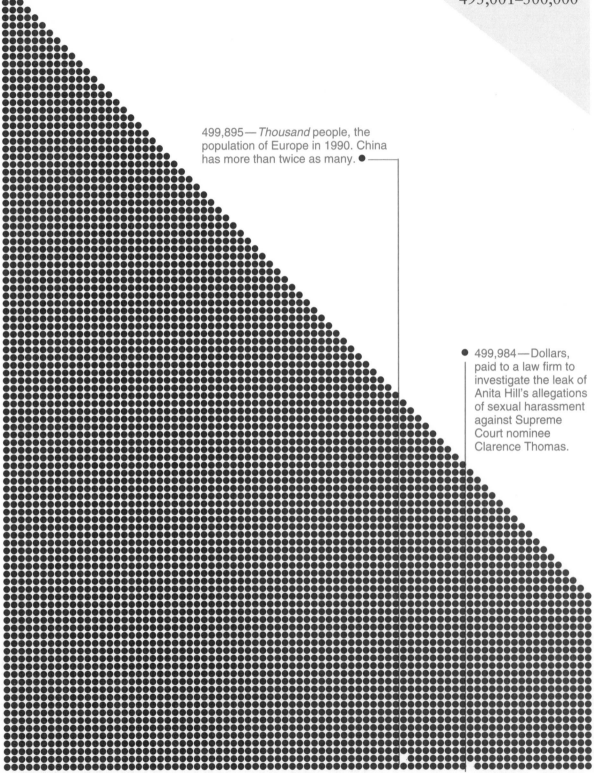

499,895—*Thousand* people, the population of Europe in 1990. China has more than twice as many. ●

● 499,984—Dollars, paid to a law firm to investigate the leak of Anita Hill's allegations of sexual harassment against Supreme Court nominee Clarence Thomas.

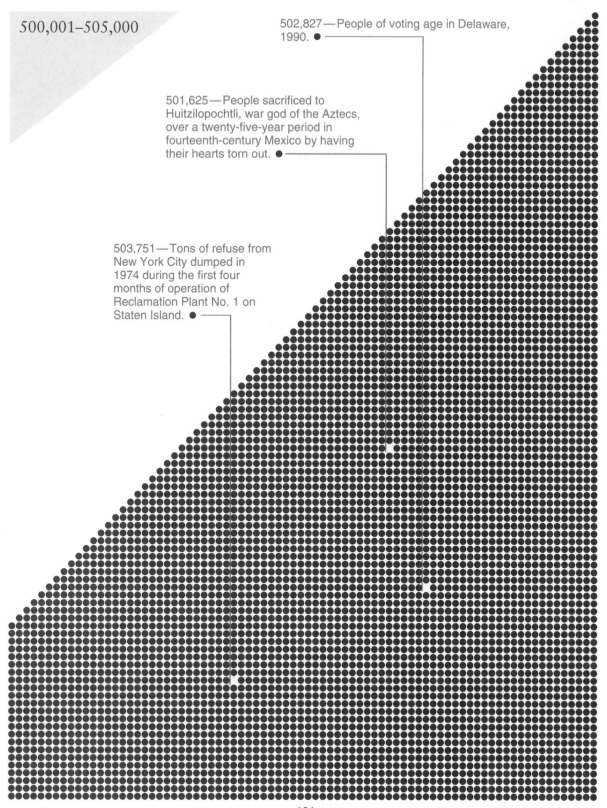

500,001–505,000

502,827—People of voting age in Delaware, 1990. ●

501,625—People sacrificed to Huitzilopochtli, war god of the Aztecs, over a twenty-five-year period in fourteenth-century Mexico by having their hearts torn out. ●

503,751—Tons of refuse from New York City dumped in 1974 during the first four months of operation of Reclamation Plant No. 1 on Staten Island. ●

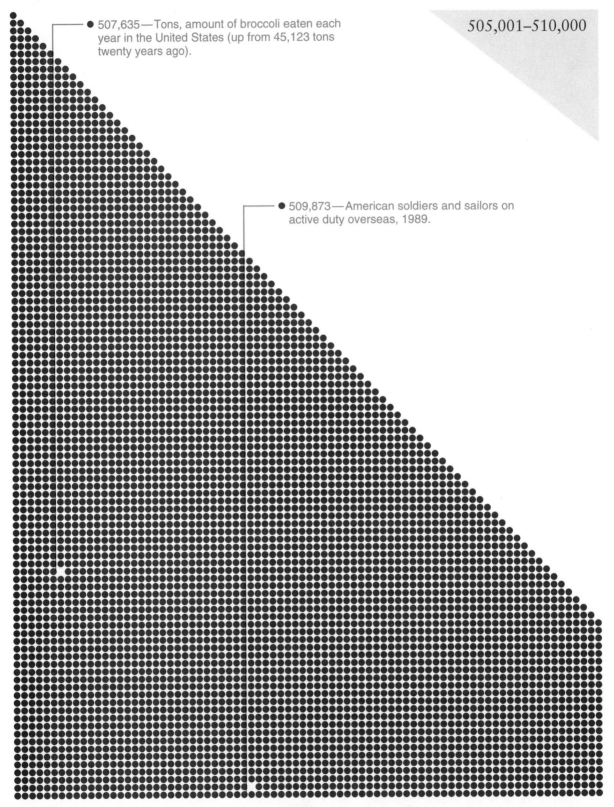

507,635—Tons, amount of broccoli eaten each year in the United States (up from 45,123 tons twenty years ago).

509,873—American soldiers and sailors on active duty overseas, 1989.

505,001–510,000

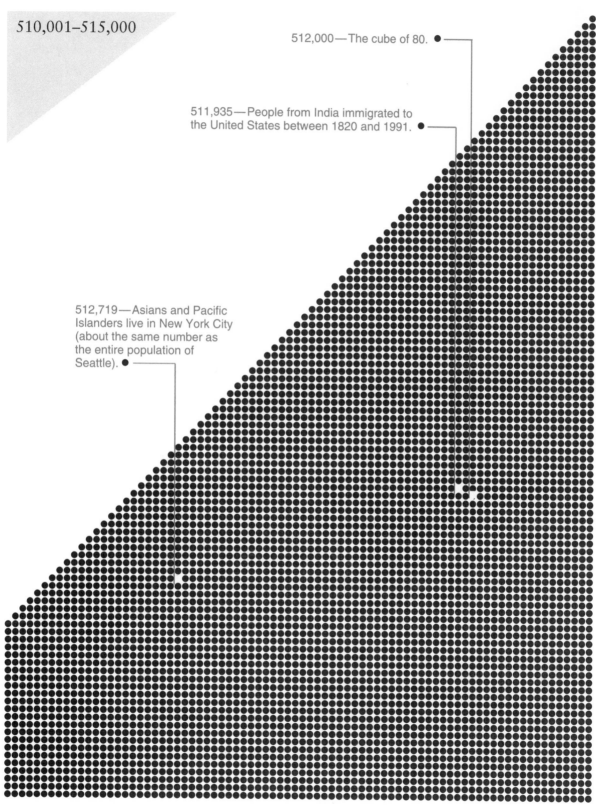

512,000—The cube of 80. ●

511,935—People from India immigrated to
the United States between 1820 and 1991. ●

512,719—Asians and Pacific
Islanders live in New York City
(about the same number as
the entire population of
Seattle). ●

516,781—Million metric tons of pig iron produced annually, worldwide.

517,000—Automobiles registered in the state of Arkansas in 1991.

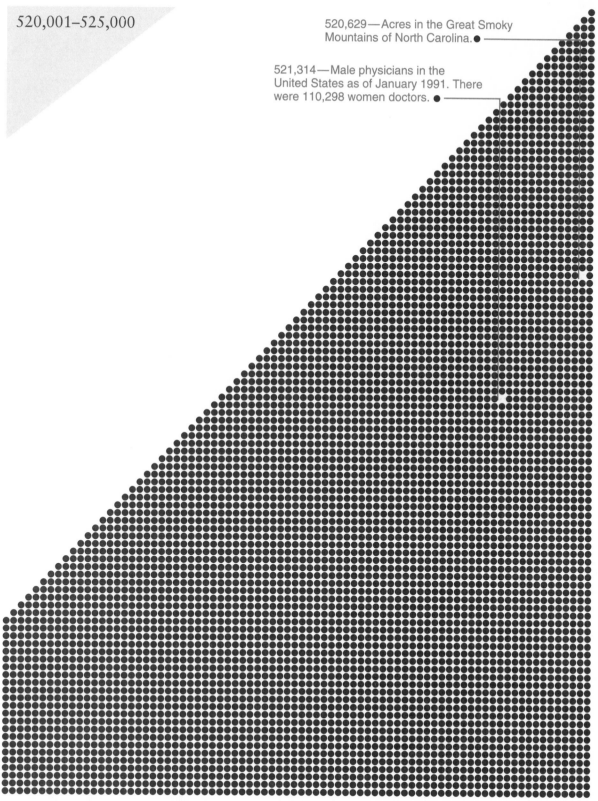

520,629—Acres in the Great Smoky Mountains of North Carolina.●

521,314—Male physicians in the United States as of January 1991. There were 110,298 women doctors. ●

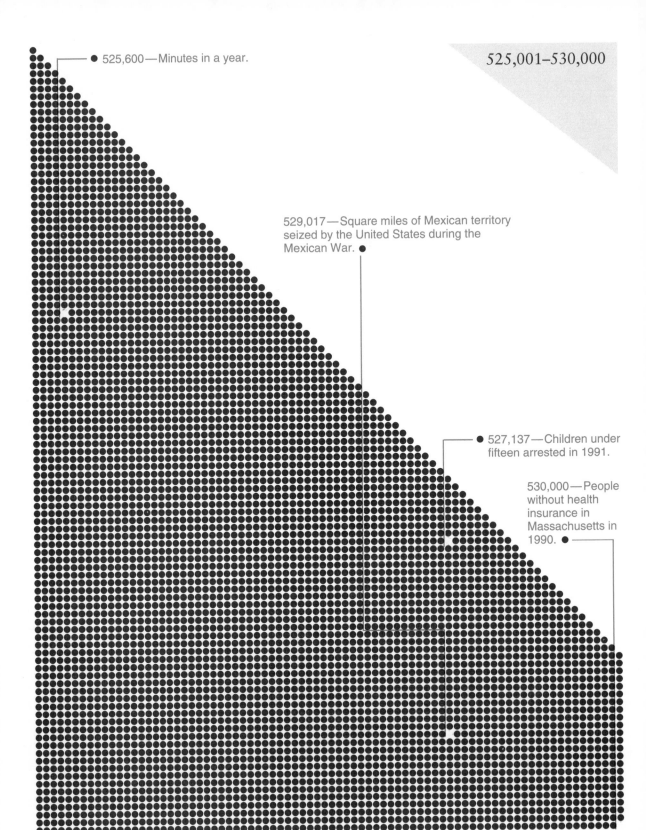

● 525,600—Minutes in a year.

529,017—Square miles of Mexican territory seized by the United States during the Mexican War. ●

● 527,137—Children under fifteen arrested in 1991.

530,000—People without health insurance in Massachusetts in 1990. ●

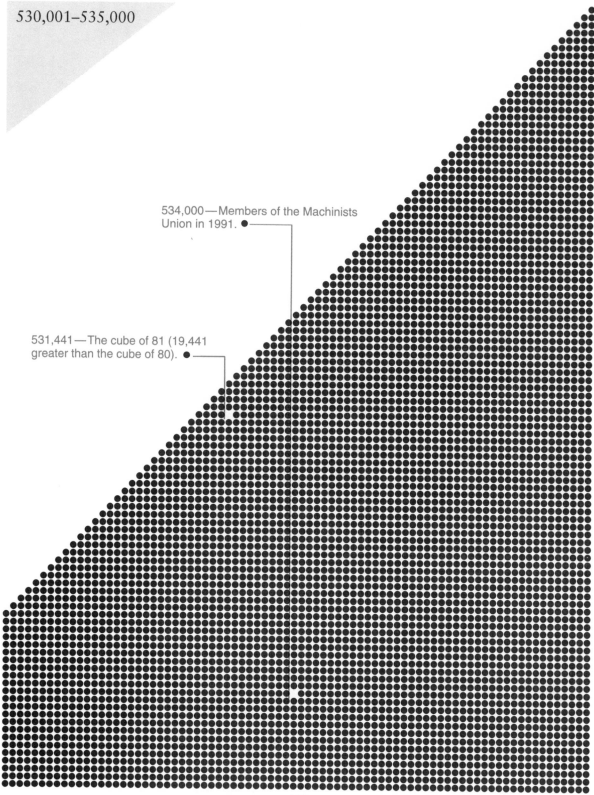

534,000—Members of the Machinists
Union in 1991. ●

531,441—The cube of 81 (19,441
greater than the cube of 80). ●

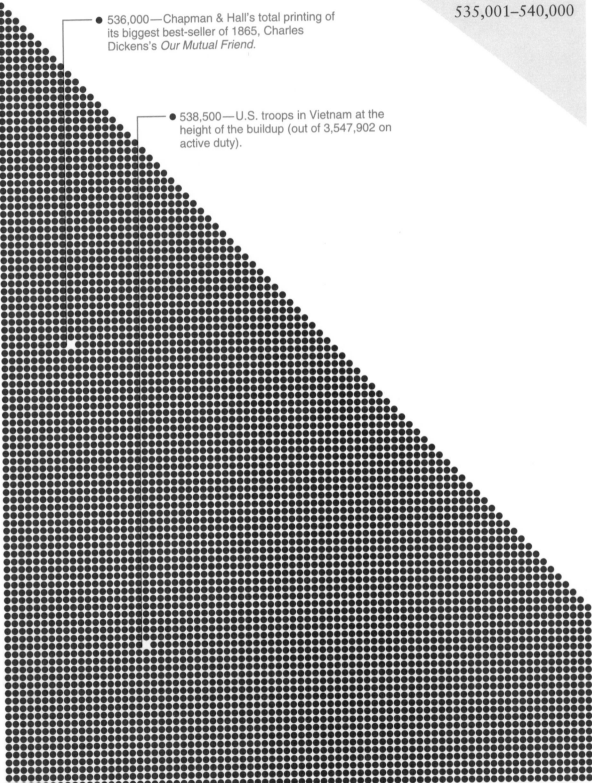

● 536,000—Chapman & Hall's total printing of its biggest best-seller of 1865, Charles Dickens's *Our Mutual Friend*.

● 538,500—U.S. troops in Vietnam at the height of the buildup (out of 3,547,902 on active duty).

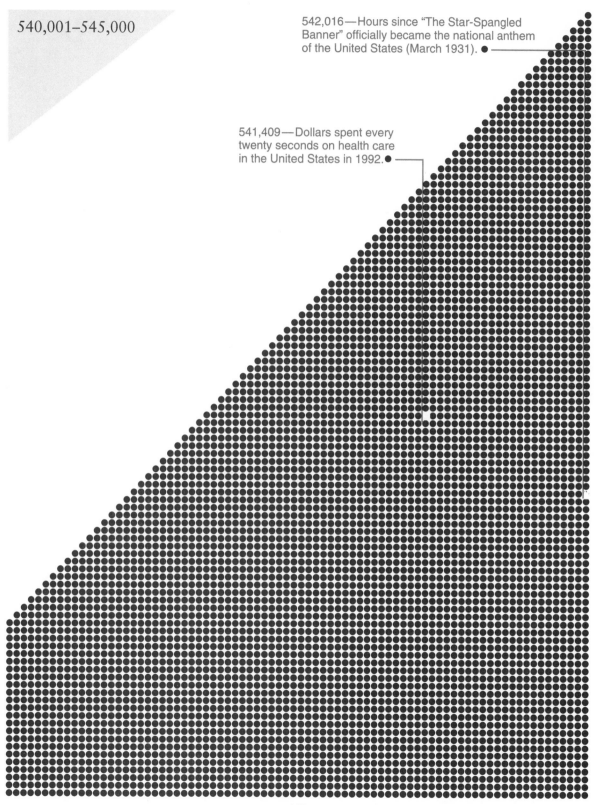

542,016—Hours since "The Star-Spangled Banner" officially became the national anthem of the United States (March 1931). ●

541,409—Dollars spent every twenty seconds on health care in the United States in 1992. ●

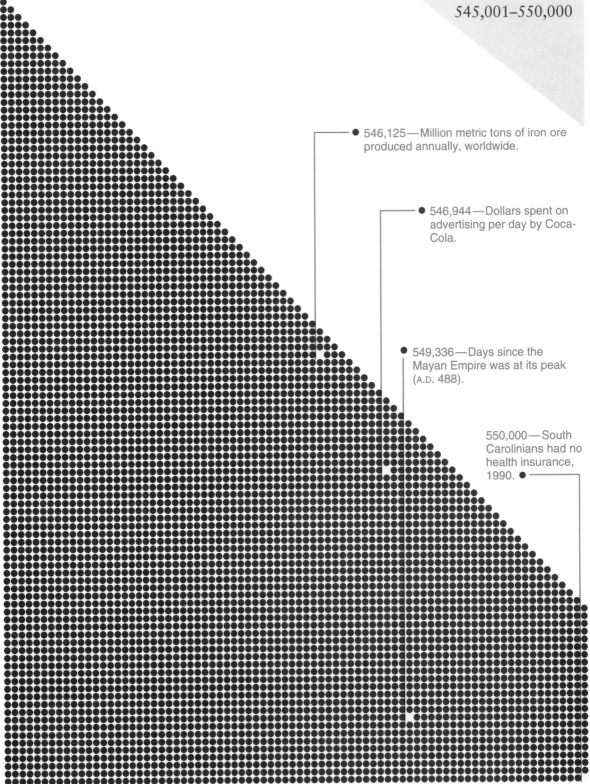

546,125—Million metric tons of iron ore produced annually, worldwide.

546,944—Dollars spent on advertising per day by Coca-Cola.

549,336—Days since the Mayan Empire was at its peak (A.D. 488).

550,000—South Carolinians had no health insurance, 1990.

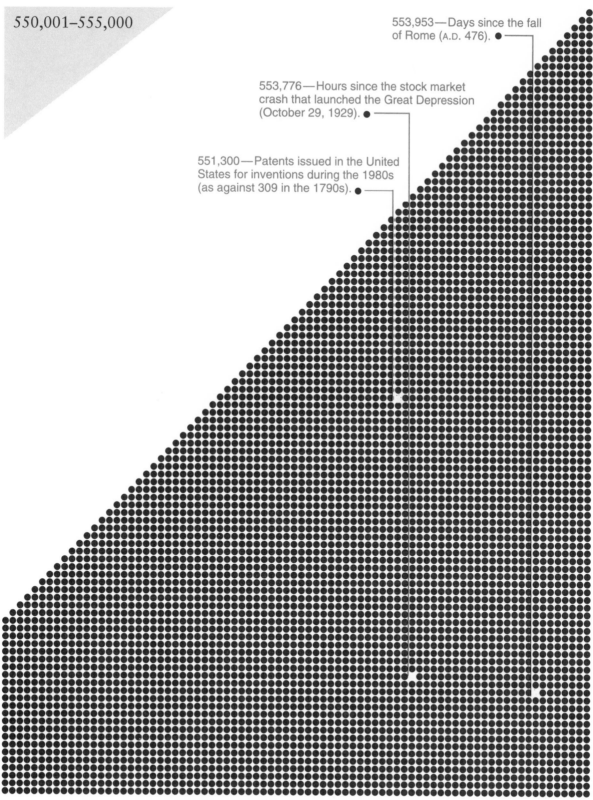

553,953—Days since the fall
of Rome (A.D. 476). ●

553,776—Hours since the stock market
crash that launched the Great Depression
(October 29, 1929). ●

551,300—Patents issued in the United
States for inventions during the 1980s
(as against 309 in the 1790s). ●

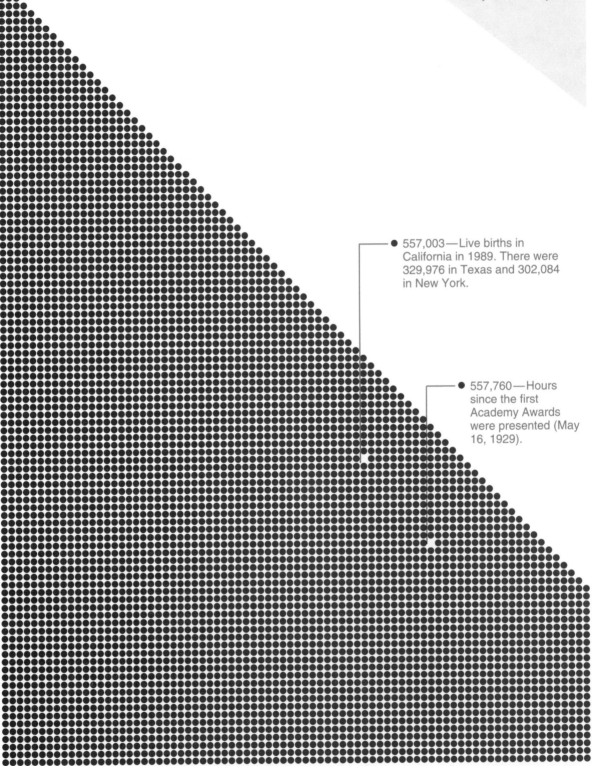

557,003—Live births in
California in 1989. There were
329,976 in Texas and 302,084
in New York.

557,760—Hours
since the first
Academy Awards
were presented (May
16, 1929).

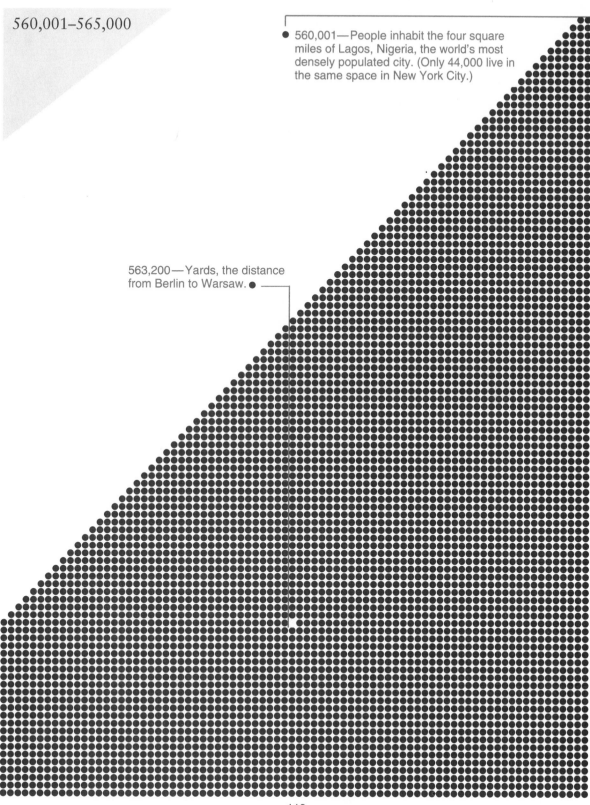

● 560,001—People inhabit the four square miles of Lagos, Nigeria, the world's most densely populated city. (Only 44,000 live in the same space in New York City.)

563,200—Yards, the distance from Berlin to Warsaw. ●

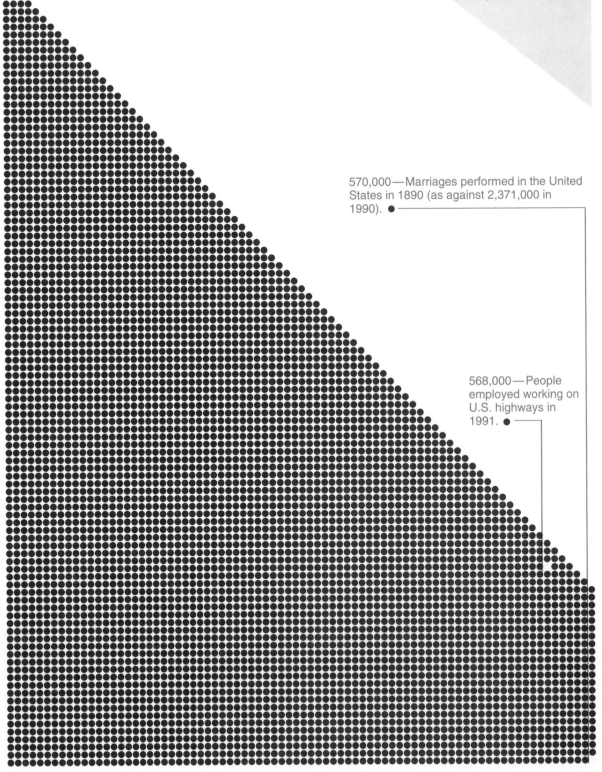

570,000—Marriages performed in the United States in 1890 (as against 2,371,000 in 1990). ●

568,000—People employed working on U.S. highways in 1991. ●

570,001–575,000

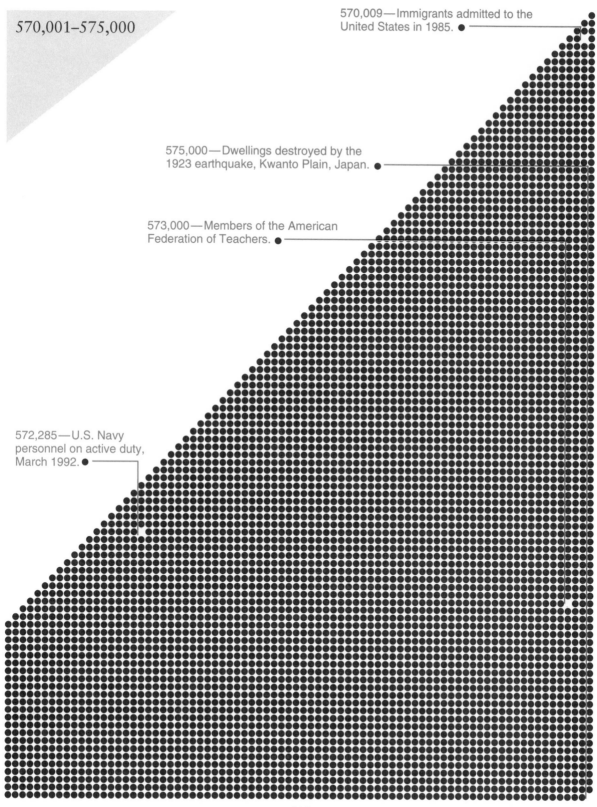

570,009—Immigrants admitted to the
United States in 1985.

575,000—Dwellings destroyed by the
1923 earthquake, Kwanto Plain, Japan.

573,000—Members of the American
Federation of Teachers.

572,285—U.S. Navy
personnel on active duty,
March 1992.

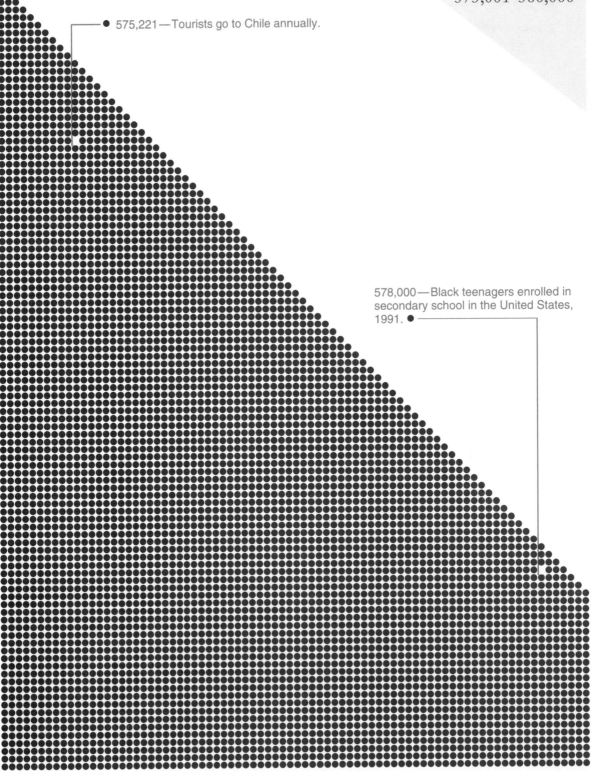

575,221—Tourists go to Chile annually.

578,000—Black teenagers enrolled in secondary school in the United States, 1991.

581,126—Black women gave birth in the United States in 1965. The total in 1988 was 671,976.

581,000—Unemployed women in the United States aged sixteen to nineteen in 1991.

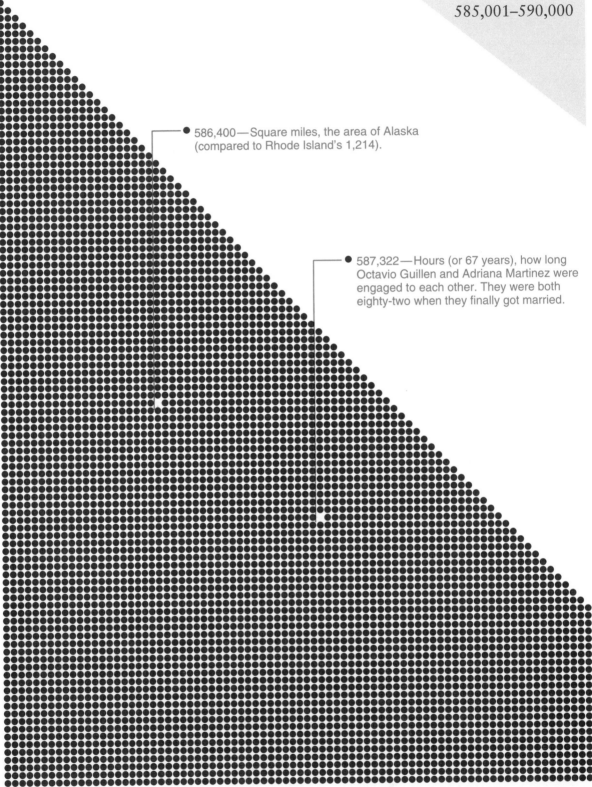

586,400—Square miles, the area of Alaska
(compared to Rhode Island's 1,214).

587,322—Hours (or 67 years), how long
Octavio Guillen and Adriana Martinez were
engaged to each other. They were both
eighty-two when they finally got married.

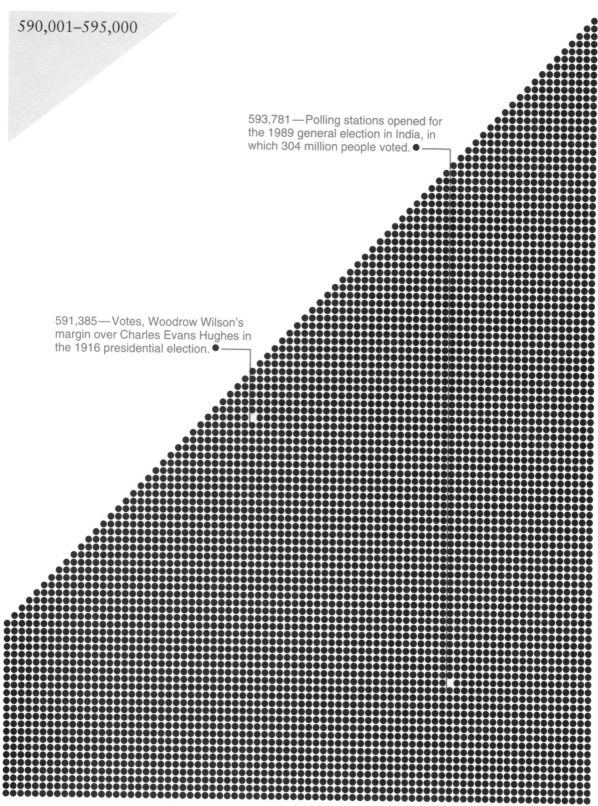

593,781—Polling stations opened for
the 1989 general election in India, in
which 304 million people voted. ●———

591,385—Votes, Woodrow Wilson's
margin over Charles Evans Hughes in
the 1916 presidential election. ●———

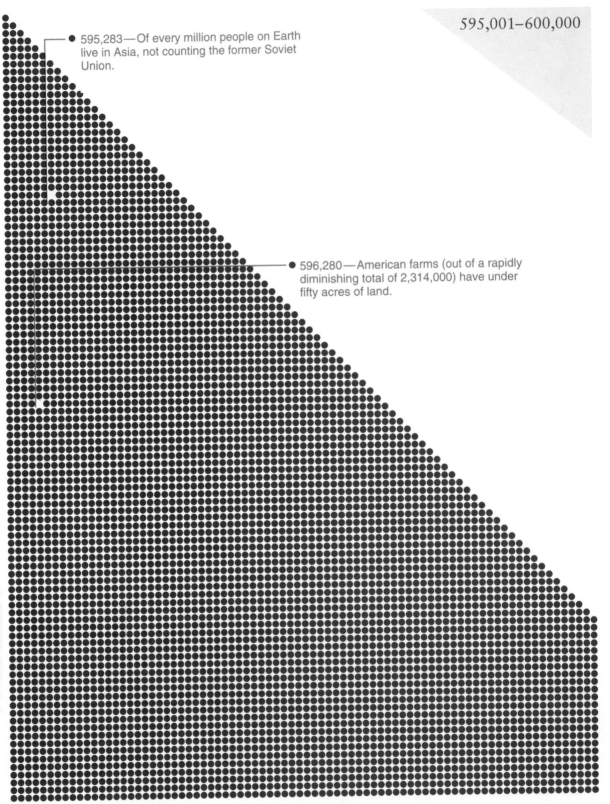

595,283—Of every million people on Earth live in Asia, not counting the former Soviet Union.

596,280—American farms (out of a rapidly diminishing total of 2,314,000) have under fifty acres of land.

600,001–605,000

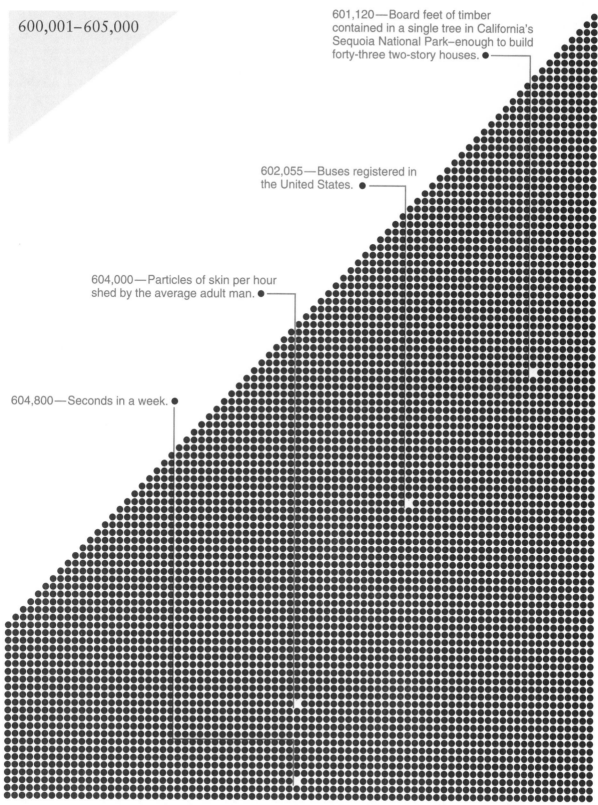

601,120—Board feet of timber contained in a single tree in California's Sequoia National Park–enough to build forty-three two-story houses. ●

602,055—Buses registered in the United States. ●

604,000—Particles of skin per hour shed by the average adult man. ●

604,800—Seconds in a week. ●

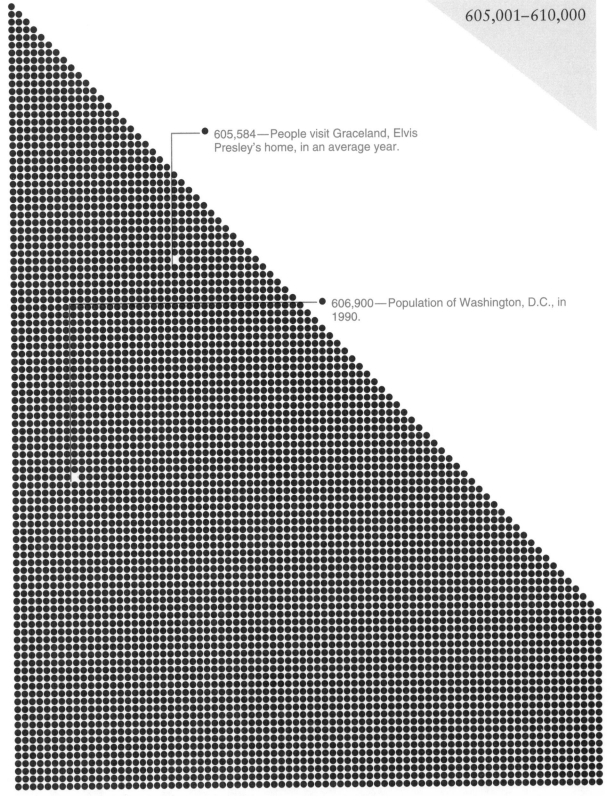

605,584—People visit Graceland, Elvis Presley's home, in an average year.

606,900—Population of Washington, D.C., in 1990.

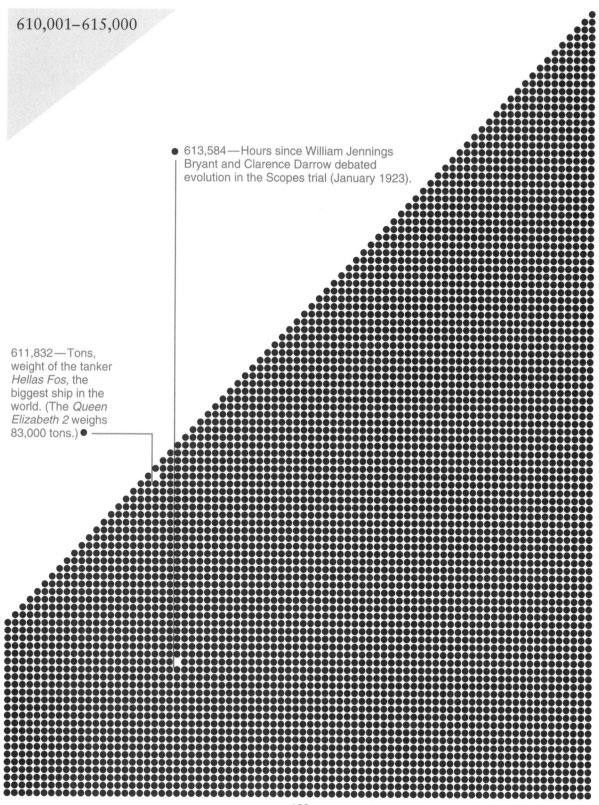

● 613,584—Hours since William Jennings
Bryant and Clarence Darrow debated
evolution in the Scopes trial (January 1923).

611,832—Tons,
weight of the tanker
Hellas Fos, the
biggest ship in the
world. (The *Queen
Elizabeth 2* weighs
83,000 tons.) ●

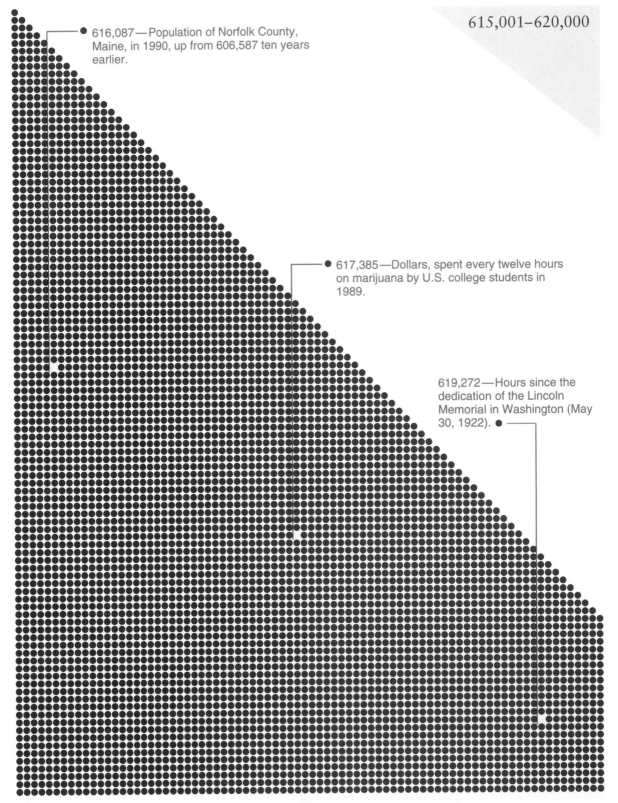

616,087—Population of Norfolk County, Maine, in 1990, up from 606,587 ten years earlier.

617,385—Dollars, spent every twelve hours on marijuana by U.S. college students in 1989.

619,272—Hours since the dedication of the Lincoln Memorial in Washington (May 30, 1922).

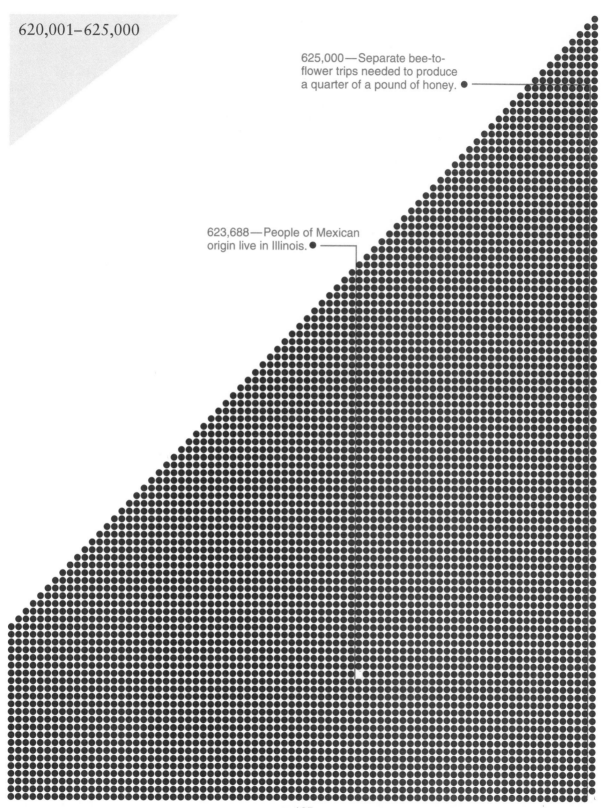

625,000—Separate bee-to-flower trips needed to produce a quarter of a pound of honey. ●

623,688—People of Mexican origin live in Illinois. ●

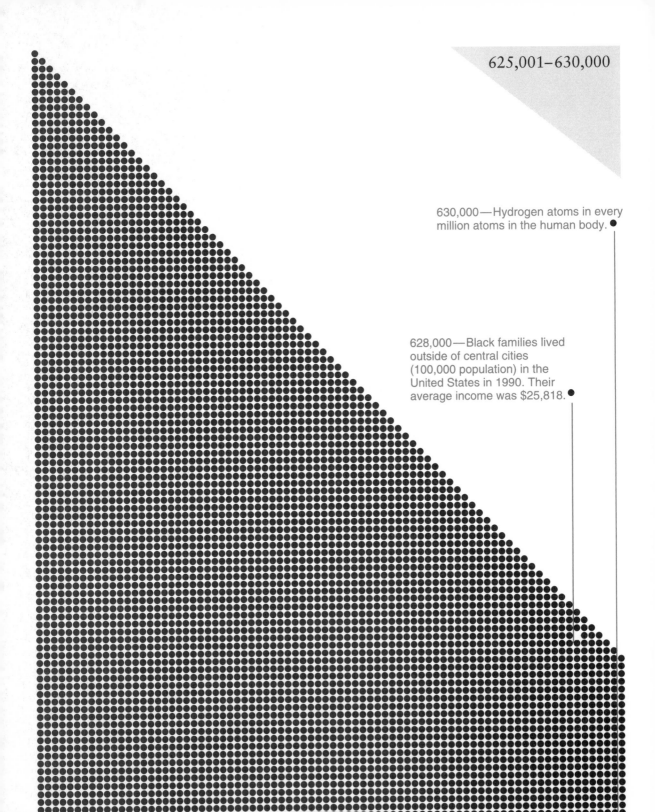

630,000—Hydrogen atoms in every
million atoms in the human body. ●

628,000—Black families lived
outside of central cities
(100,000 population) in the
United States in 1990. Their
average income was $25,818. ●

632,772—Population of Hawaii in 1960. (It
had nearly doubled, to 1,109,229, by 1990.) ●

632,000—Dollars of undocumented
expenses found in a Federal Election
Commission audit of the 1988 Jesse Jackson
campaign. The FEC voted to seek $311,000
from the Jackson campaign. ●

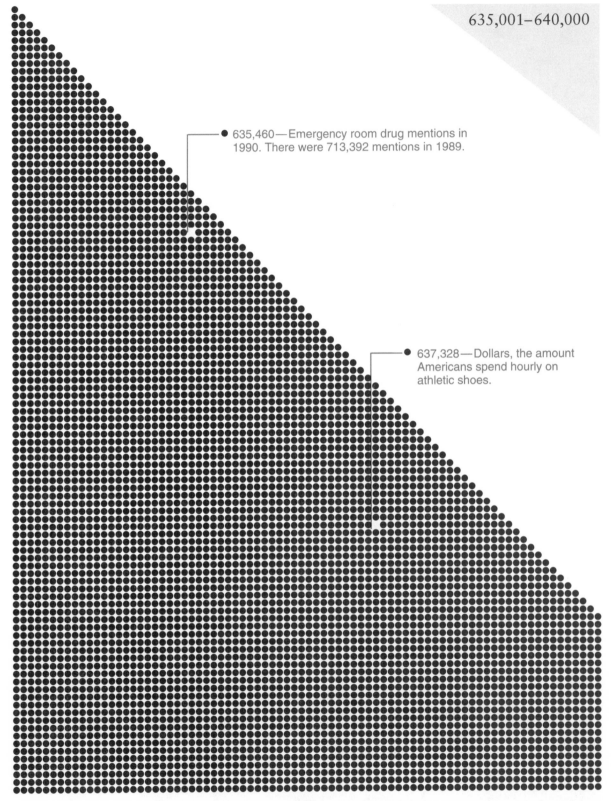

635,460—Emergency room drug mentions in 1990. There were 713,392 mentions in 1989.

637,328—Dollars, the amount Americans spend hourly on athletic shoes.

642,993—Bankruptcy petitions filed in the United States in 1989, up from 360,329 in 1981. ●

644,738—Daily circulation of the *New York Post*. ●

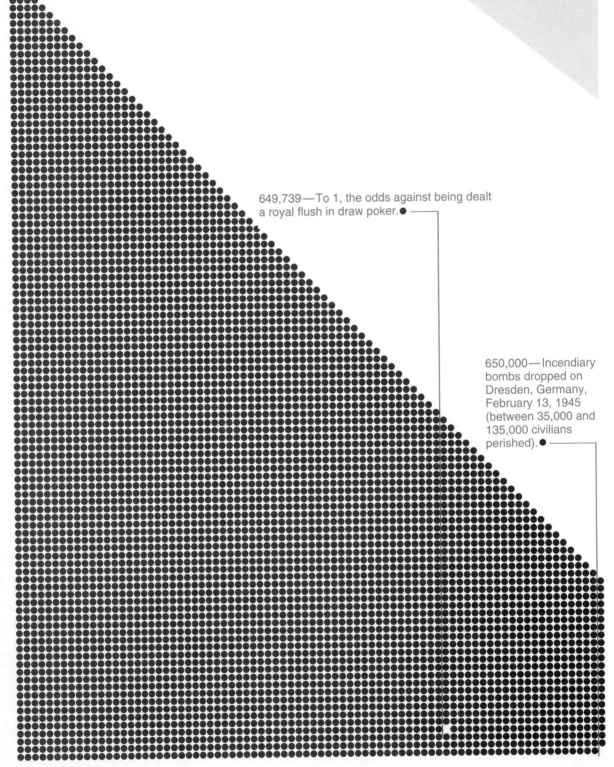

649,739—To 1, the odds against being dealt a royal flush in draw poker.●

650,000—Incendiary bombs dropped on Dresden, Germany, February 13, 1945 (between 35,000 and 135,000 civilians perished).●

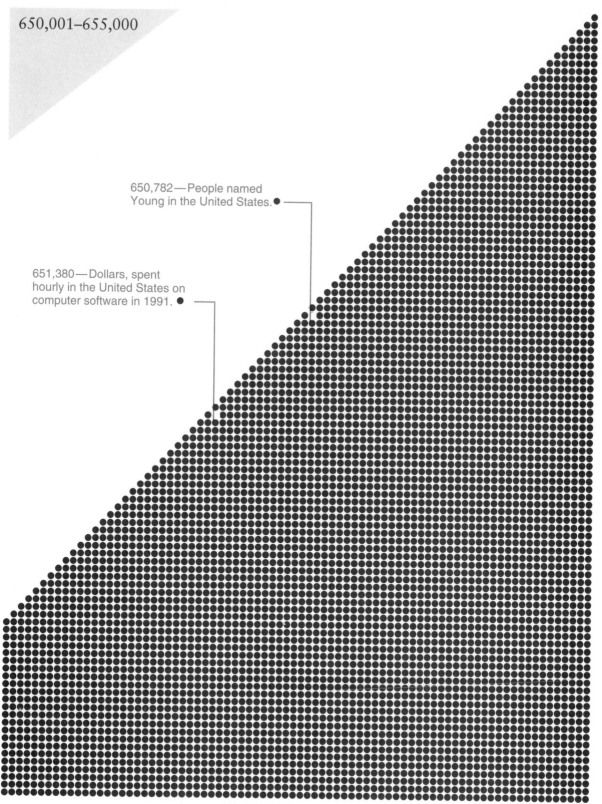

650,782—People named
Young in the United States.

651,380—Dollars, spent
hourly in the United States on
computer software in 1991.

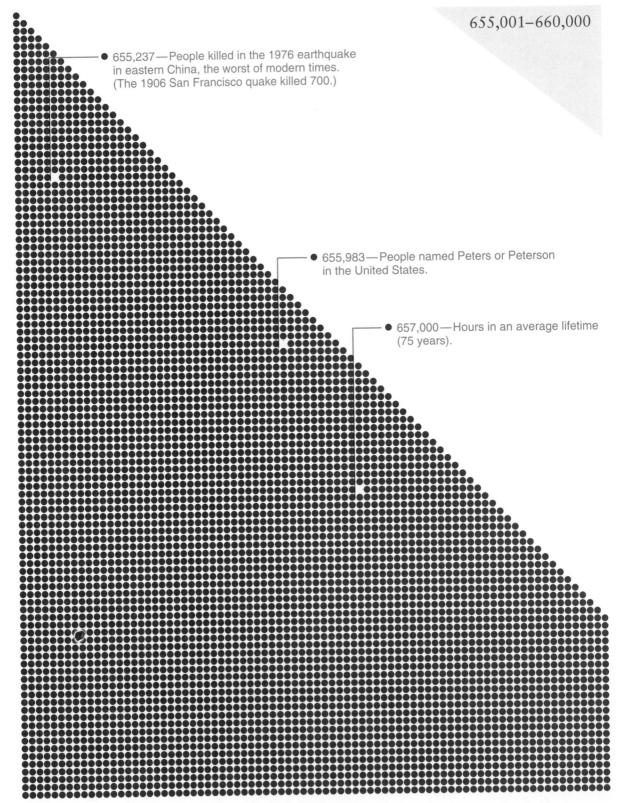

655,237—People killed in the 1976 earthquake in eastern China, the worst of modern times. (The 1906 San Francisco quake killed 700.)

655,983—People named Peters or Peterson in the United States.

657,000—Hours in an average lifetime (75 years).

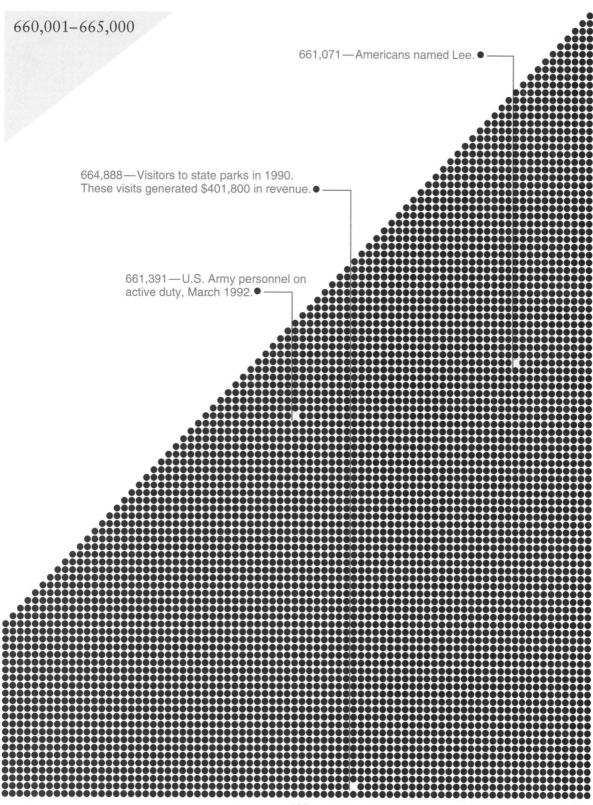

661,071—Americans named Lee. ●

664,888—Visitors to state parks in 1990.
These visits generated $401,800 in revenue. ●

661,391—U.S. Army personnel on
active duty, March 1992. ●

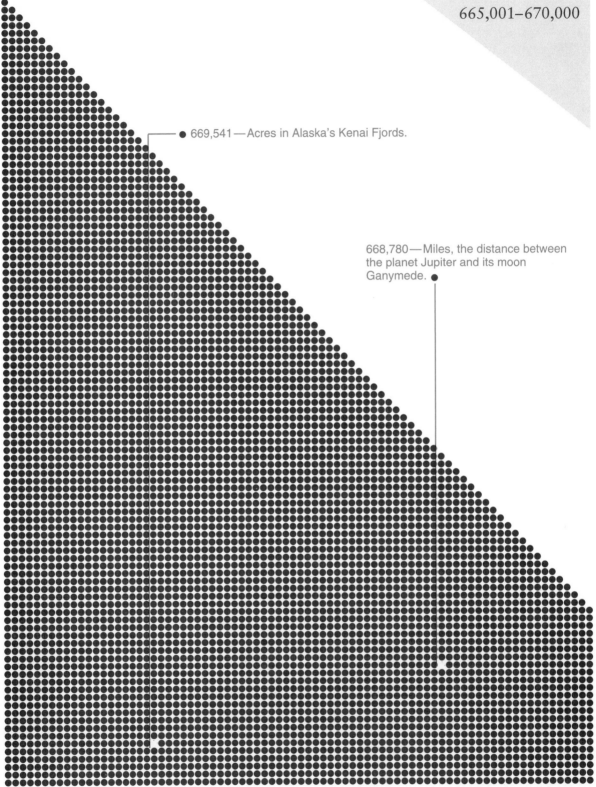

● 669,541—Acres in Alaska's Kenai Fjords.

668,780—Miles, the distance between the planet Jupiter and its moon Ganymede. ●

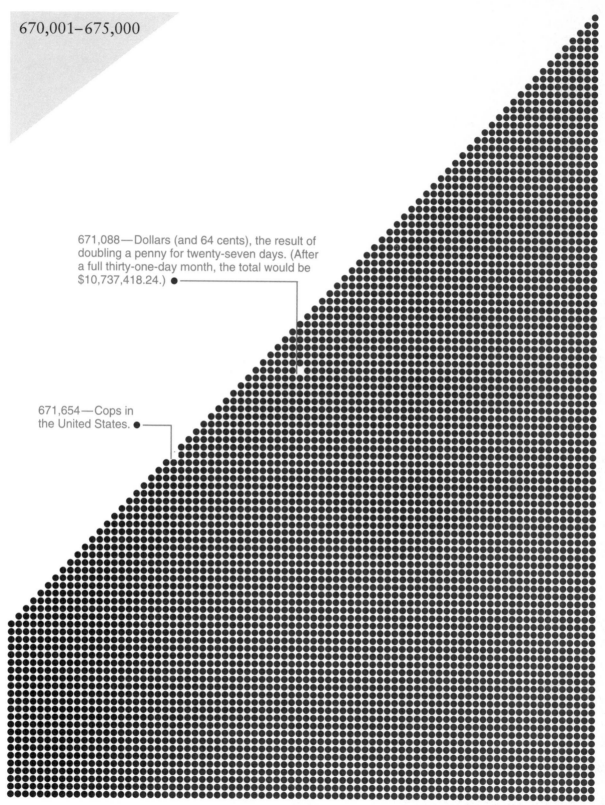

671,088—Dollars (and 64 cents), the result of
doubling a penny for twenty-seven days. (After
a full thirty-one-day month, the total would be
$10,737,418.24.) ●

671,654—Cops in
the United States. ●

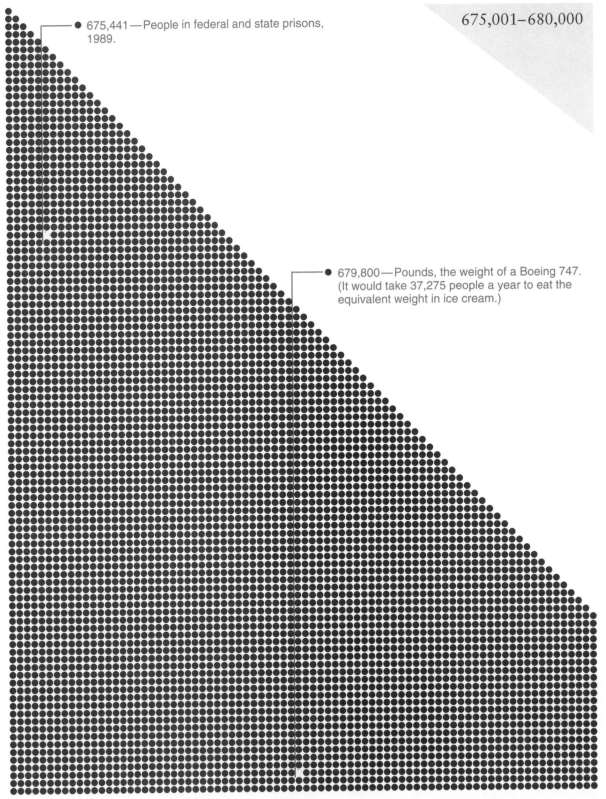

675,441—People in federal and state prisons, 1989.

675,001–680,000

679,800—Pounds, the weight of a Boeing 747. (It would take 37,275 people a year to eat the equivalent weight in ice cream.)

683,000—Women were raped in the United
States in 1990, according to a National Institute
on Drug Abuse study. This figure is five times
the estimate of other government studies. ●

684,932—New cases of
sexually transmitted infections
per day, worldwide. (Of these,
5,708 are HIV.)

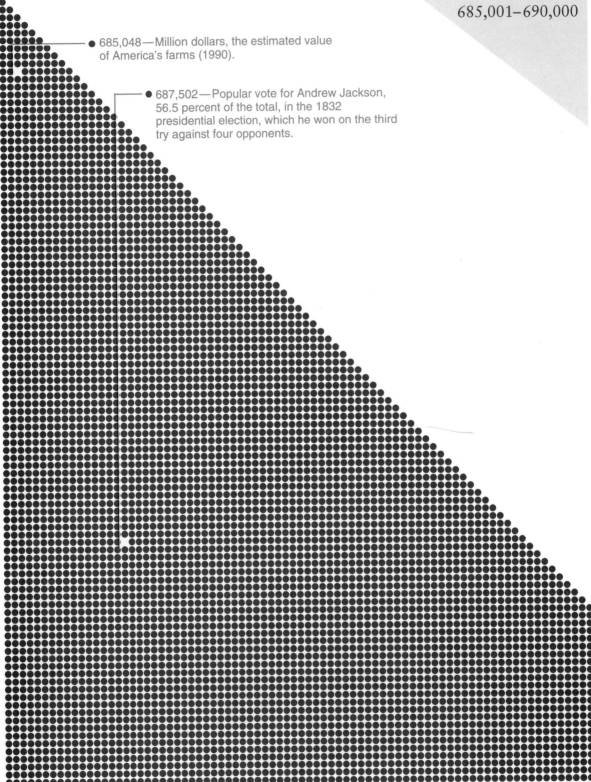

685,048—Million dollars, the estimated value of America's farms (1990).

687,502—Popular vote for Andrew Jackson, 56.5 percent of the total, in the 1832 presidential election, which he won on the third try against four opponents.

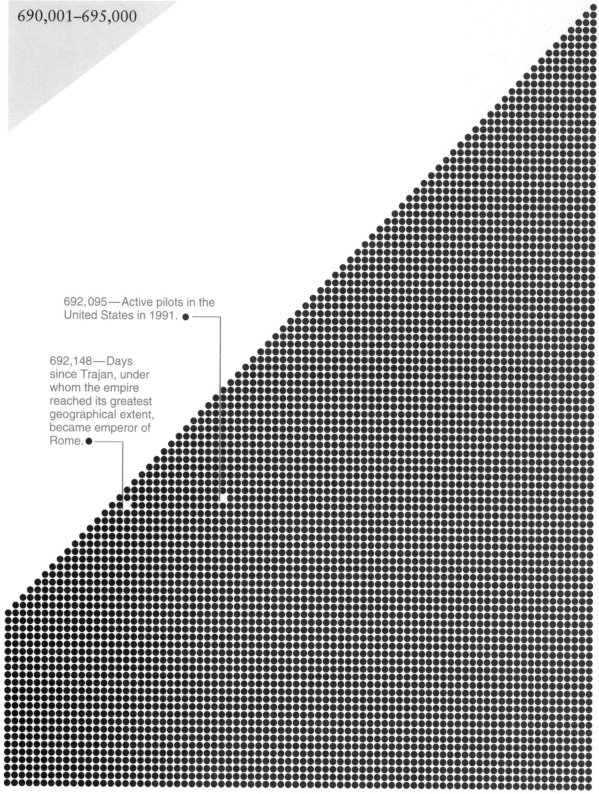

692,095—Active pilots in the United States in 1991.

692,148—Days since Trajan, under whom the empire reached its greatest geographical extent, became emperor of Rome.

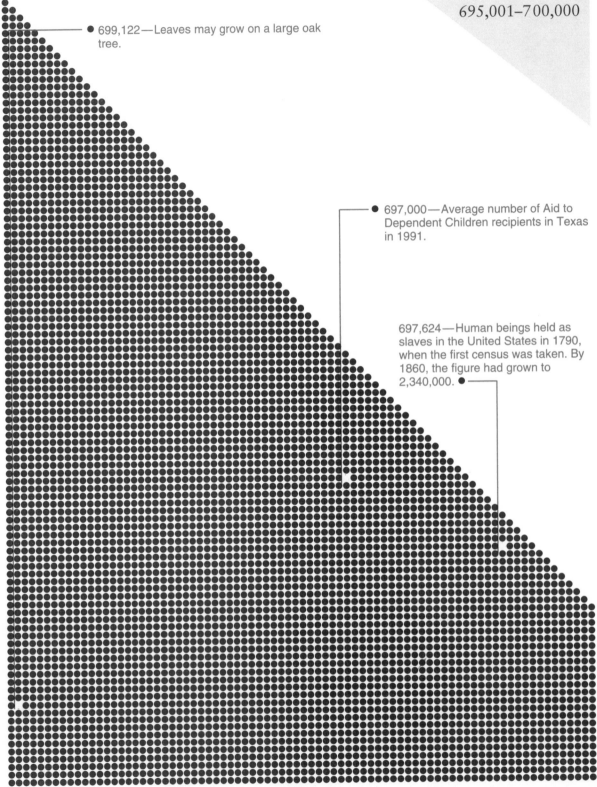

699,122—Leaves may grow on a large oak tree.

697,000—Average number of Aid to Dependent Children recipients in Texas in 1991.

697,624—Human beings held as slaves in the United States in 1790, when the first census was taken. By 1860, the figure had grown to 2,340,000.

700,001–705,000

700,739—Circulation of the Atlanta Sunday *Journal & Constitution.* The population of the city itself is only 394,000. ●

703,475—Dollars, spent every ten minutes in the United States on tobacco. ●

704,604—Number of visits to U.S. physicians yearly for the twenty primary reasons for seeing a doctor.

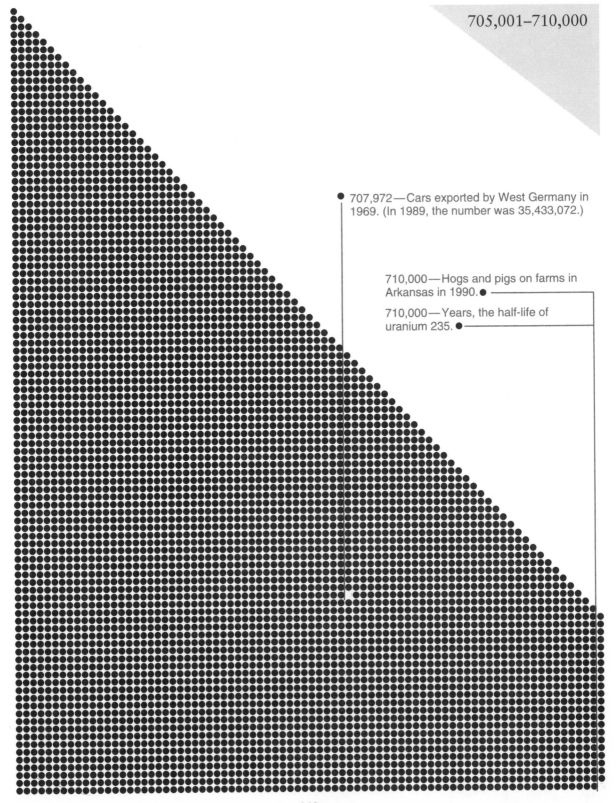

707,972—Cars exported by West Germany in 1969. (In 1989, the number was 35,433,072.)

710,000—Hogs and pigs on farms in Arkansas in 1990.

710,000—Years, the half-life of uranium 235.

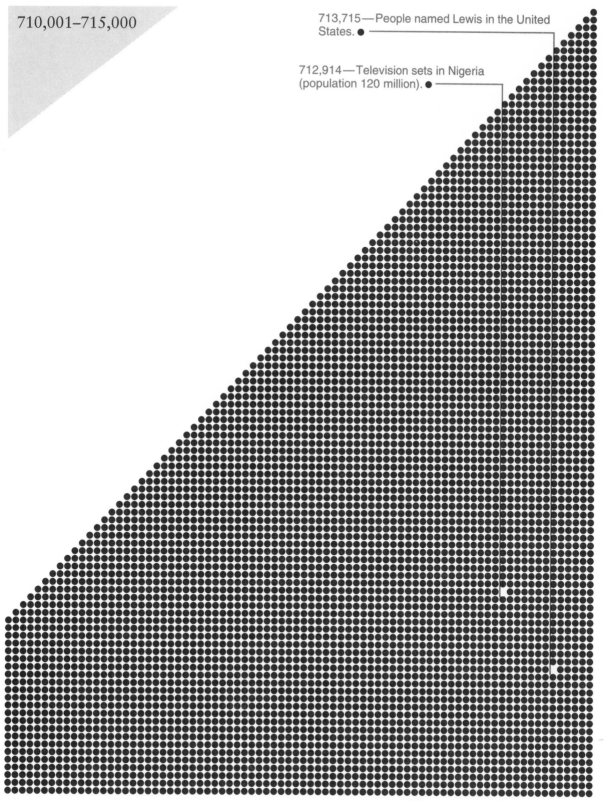

710,001–715,000

713,715—People named Lewis in the United States. ●

712,914—Television sets in Nigeria (population 120 million). ●

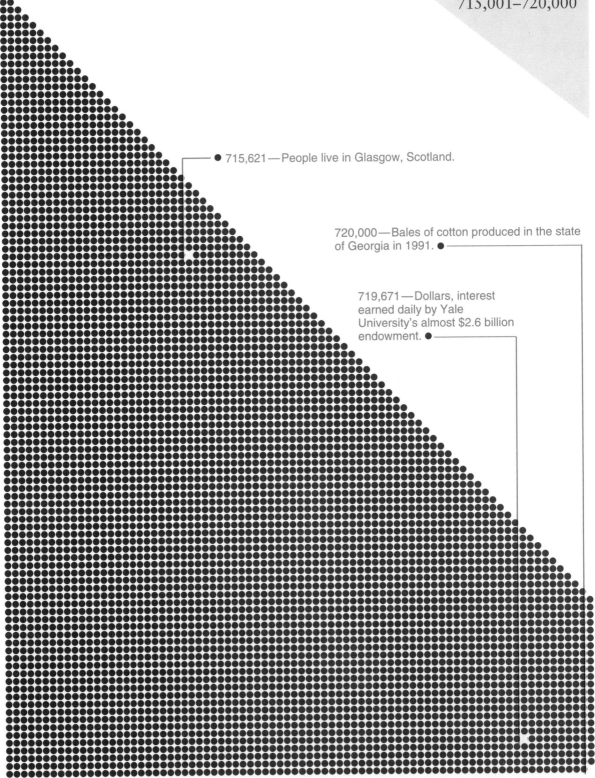

715,621 — People live in Glasgow, Scotland.

720,000 — Bales of cotton produced in the state of Georgia in 1991.

719,671 — Dollars, interest earned daily by Yale University's almost $2.6 billion endowment.

720,001–725,000

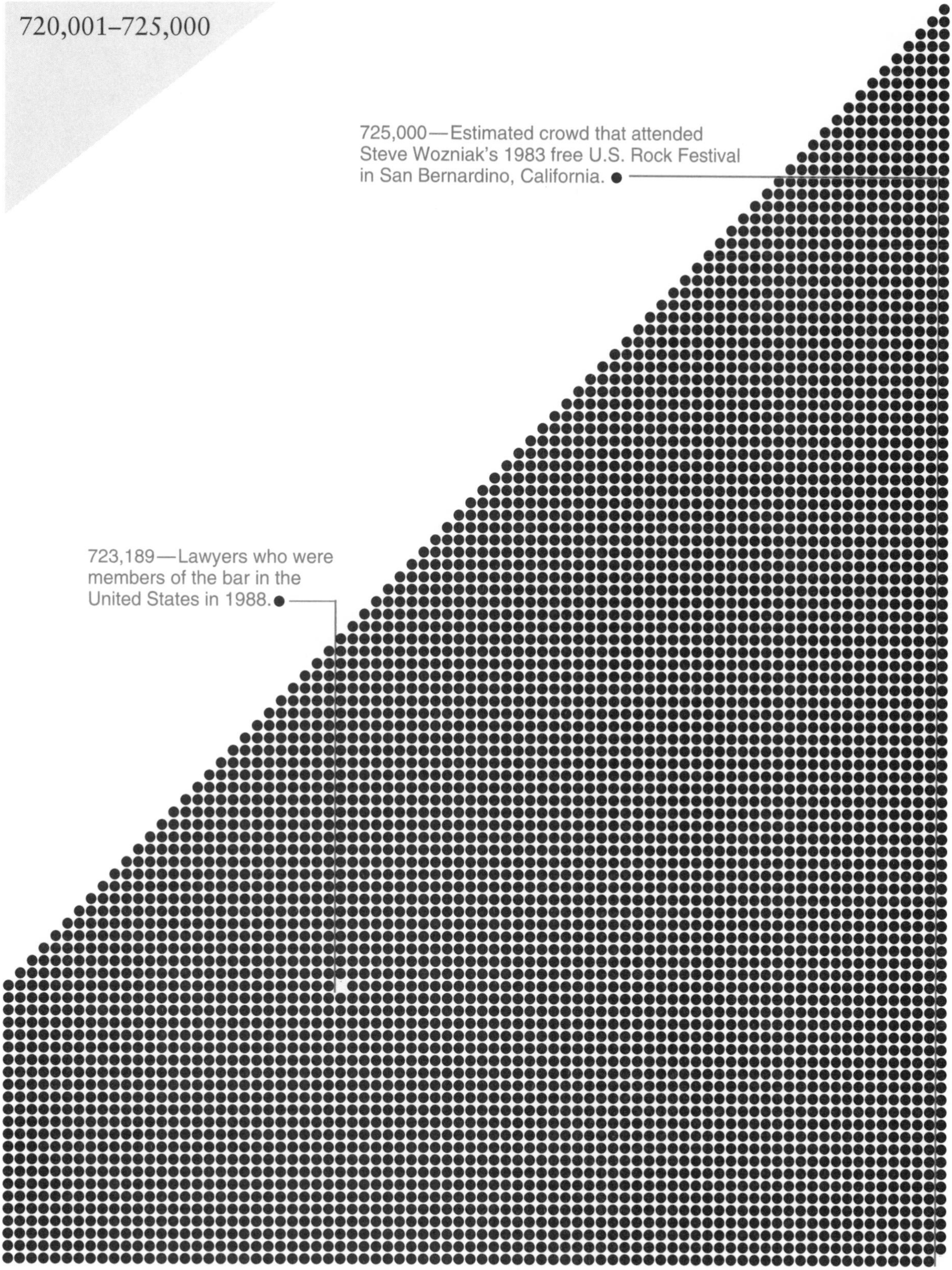
725,000—Estimated crowd that attended Steve Wozniak's 1983 free U.S. Rock Festival in San Bernardino, California.
723,189—Lawyers who were members of the bar in the United States in 1988.

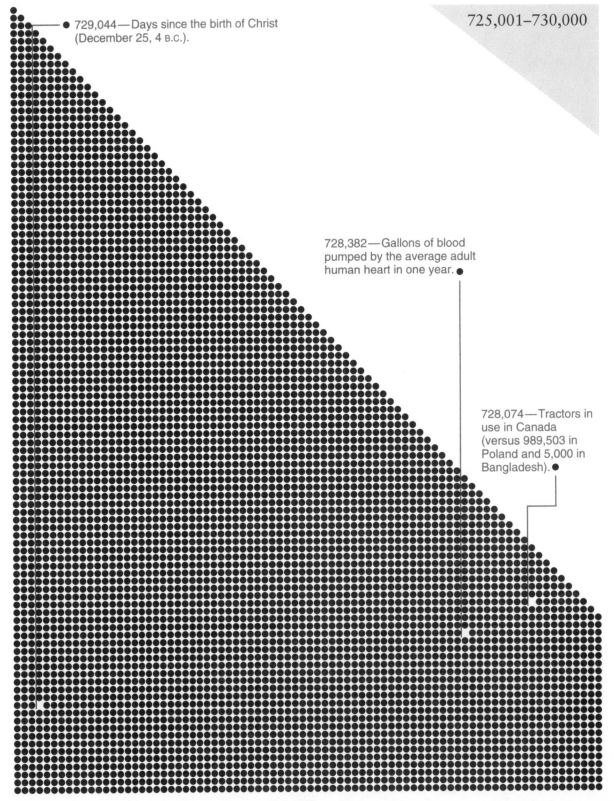

729,044—Days since the birth of Christ (December 25, 4 B.C.).

728,382—Gallons of blood pumped by the average adult human heart in one year. ●

728,074—Tractors in use in Canada (versus 989,503 in Poland and 5,000 in Bangladesh). ●

146

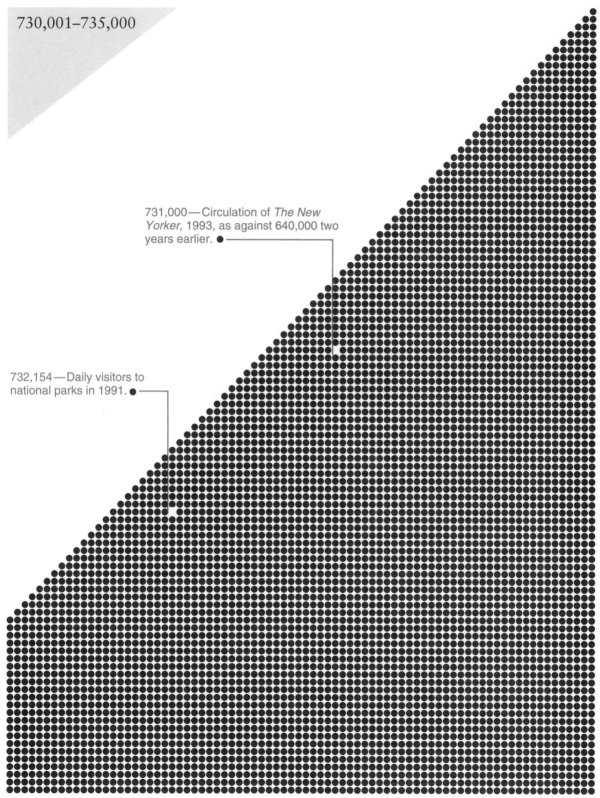

731,000—Circulation of *The New Yorker,* 1993, as against 640,000 two years earlier. ●

732,154—Daily visitors to national parks in 1991. ●

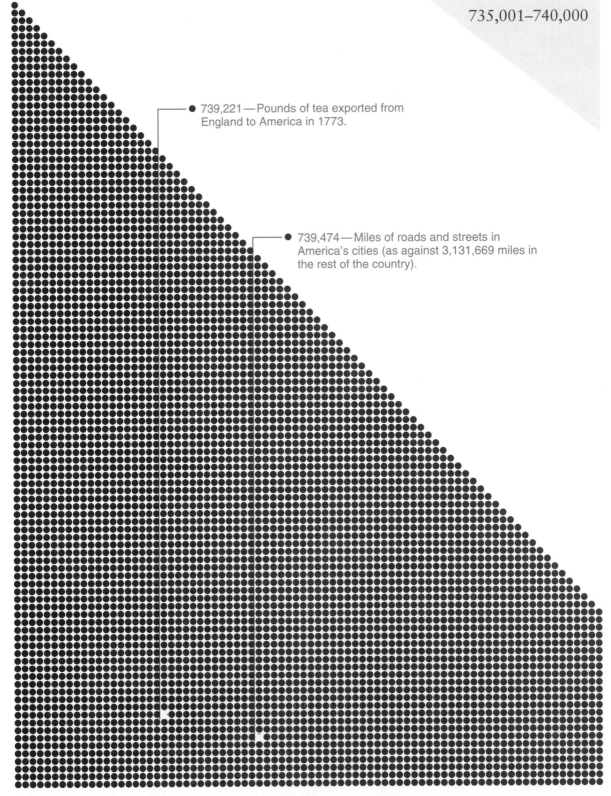

739,221—Pounds of tea exported from England to America in 1773.

739,474—Miles of roads and streets in America's cities (as against 3,131,669 miles in the rest of the country).

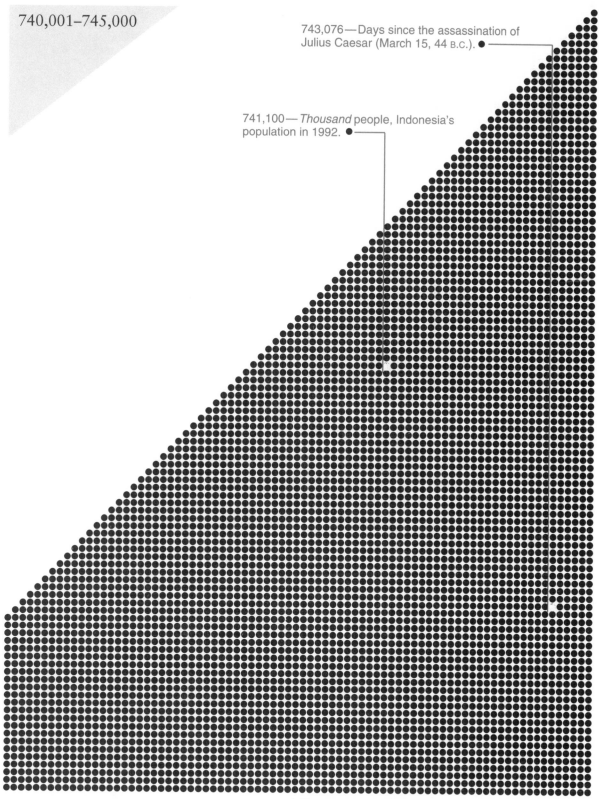

743,076—Days since the assassination of Julius Caesar (March 15, 44 B.C.). ●

741,100— *Thousand* people, Indonesia's population in 1992. ●

745,128—Miles, distance traveled by a beam
of light in four seconds (more than three times
the distance from the Earth to the Moon).

747,500—Dollars a year, average pay for an
American CEO.

750,001–755,000

753,876—Hours, the length of time Sir Temulji Bhicaji Nariman and Lady Nariman were married. They married at age five and stayed that way from 1853 to 1940, when he died. ●

751,802—Trips to Switzerland are made by Americans each year. (Almost 15 million trips are made to Mexico.) ●

751,000—Hispanic families lived below the poverty line in the United States in 1979. The number in 1990 was 1,244,000. ●

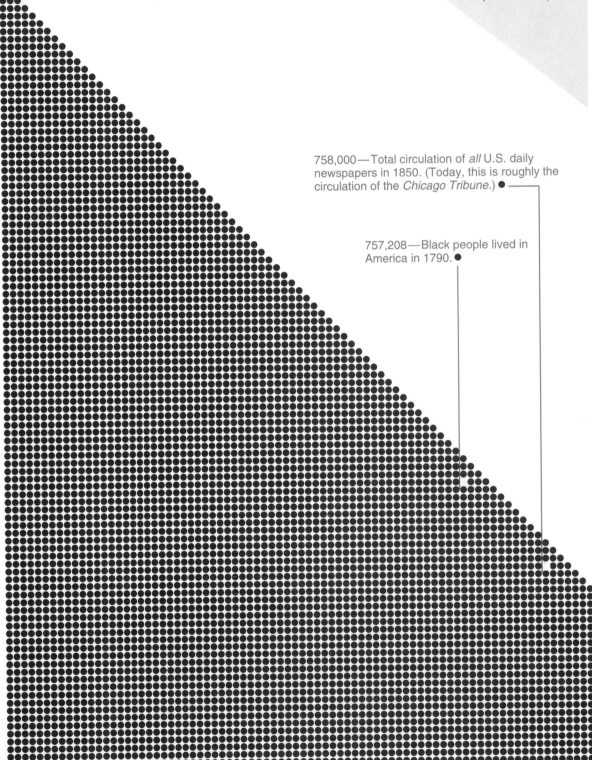

758,000—Total circulation of *all* U.S. daily newspapers in 1850. (Today, this is roughly the circulation of the *Chicago Tribune*.) ●

757,208—Black people lived in America in 1790. ●

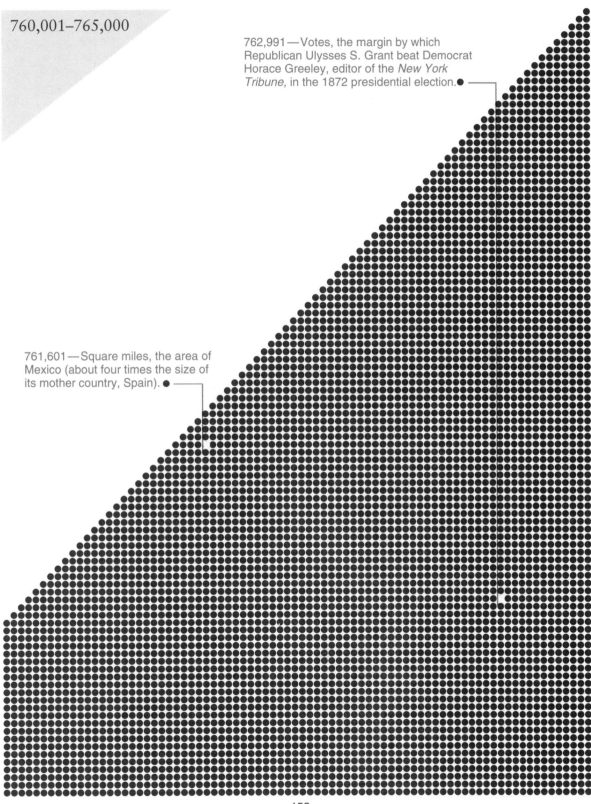

760,001–765,000

762,991—Votes, the margin by which Republican Ulysses S. Grant beat Democrat Horace Greeley, editor of the *New York Tribune,* in the 1872 presidential election.●

761,601—Square miles, the area of Mexico (about four times the size of its mother country, Spain). ●

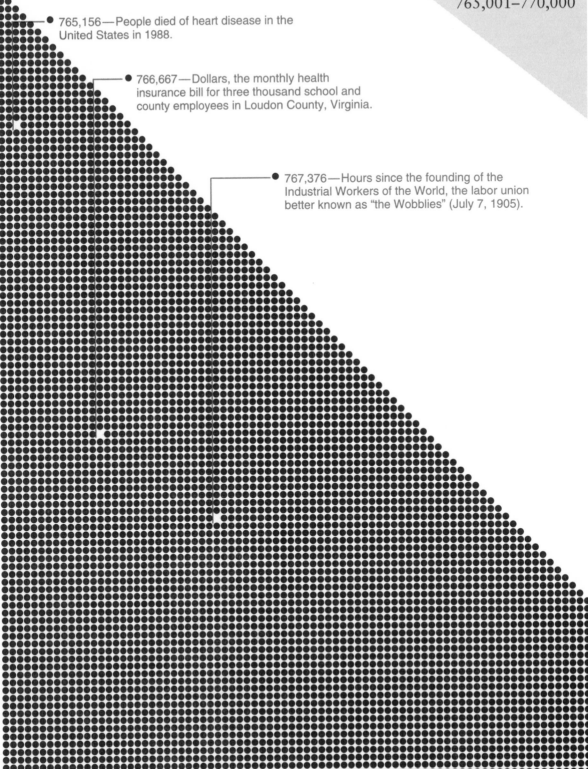

765,156—People died of heart disease in the United States in 1988.

766,667—Dollars, the monthly health insurance bill for three thousand school and county employees in Loudon County, Virginia.

767,376—Hours since the founding of the Industrial Workers of the World, the labor union better known as "the Wobblies" (July 7, 1905).

771,354—Fords produced in
the United States in 1991. ●

773,692—Words, the length of the Bible. ●

774,900—Square feet, the size of the Imperial
Palace in Beijing, China, the world's largest
palace. ●

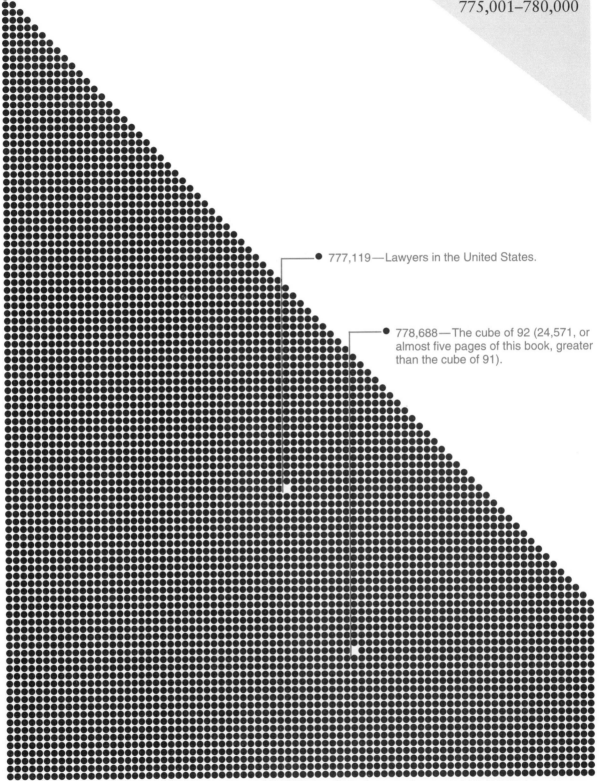

777,119—Lawyers in the United States.

778,688—The cube of 92 (24,571, or almost five pages of this book, greater than the cube of 91).

781,270—Days since the Romans destroyed
Carthage in the Third Punic War. ●

781,250—Sparrows, the progeny of
two parent birds after eight years' time
(given optimum survival conditions). ●

780,880—Parts per million of nitrogen in air. ●

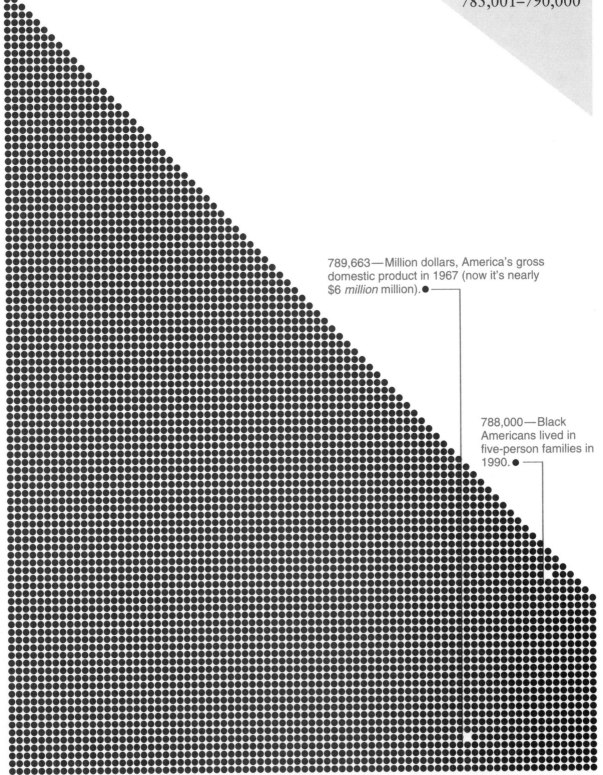

789,663—Million dollars, America's gross
domestic product in 1967 (now it's nearly
$6 *million* million).●——

788,000—Black
Americans lived in
five-person families in
1990.●——

158

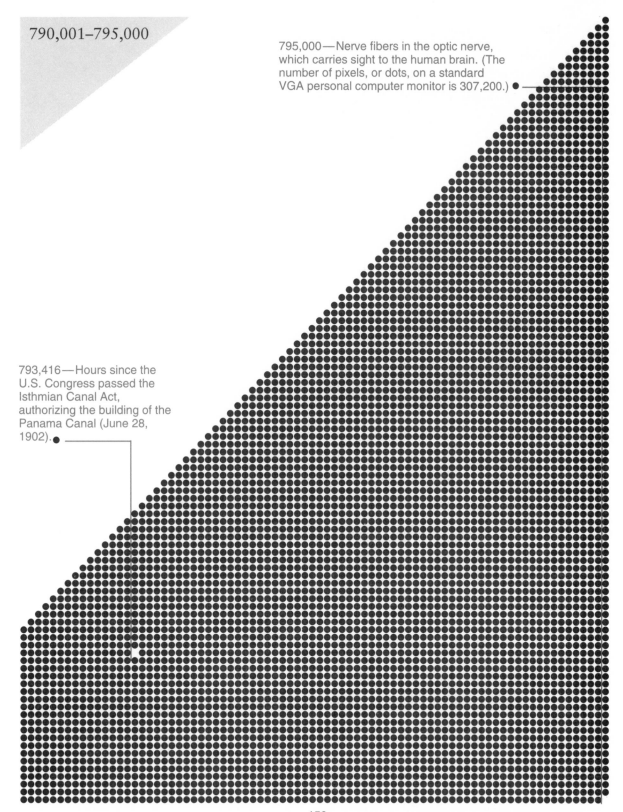

795,000—Nerve fibers in the optic nerve, which carries sight to the human brain. (The number of pixels, or dots, on a standard VGA personal computer monitor is 307,200.)

793,416—Hours since the U.S. Congress passed the Isthmian Canal Act, authorizing the building of the Panama Canal (June 28, 1902).

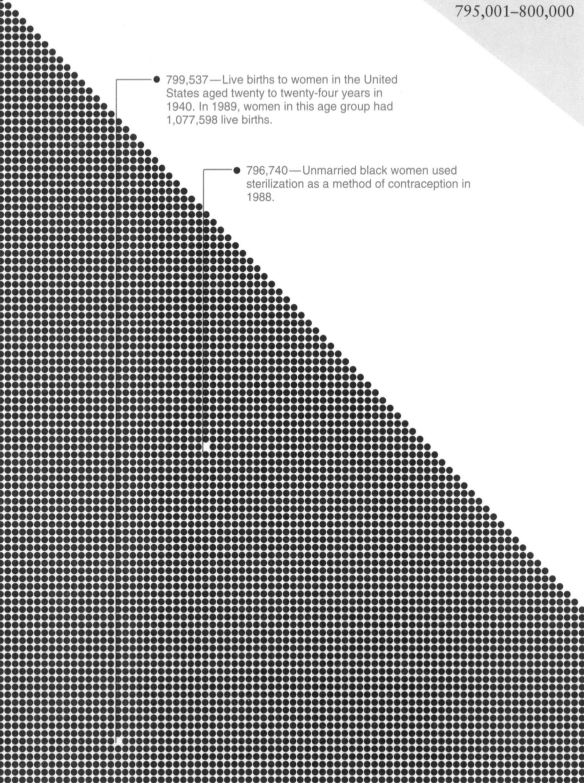

799,537—Live births to women in the United States aged twenty to twenty-four years in 1940. In 1989, women in this age group had 1,077,598 live births.

796,740—Unmarried black women used sterilization as a method of contraception in 1988.

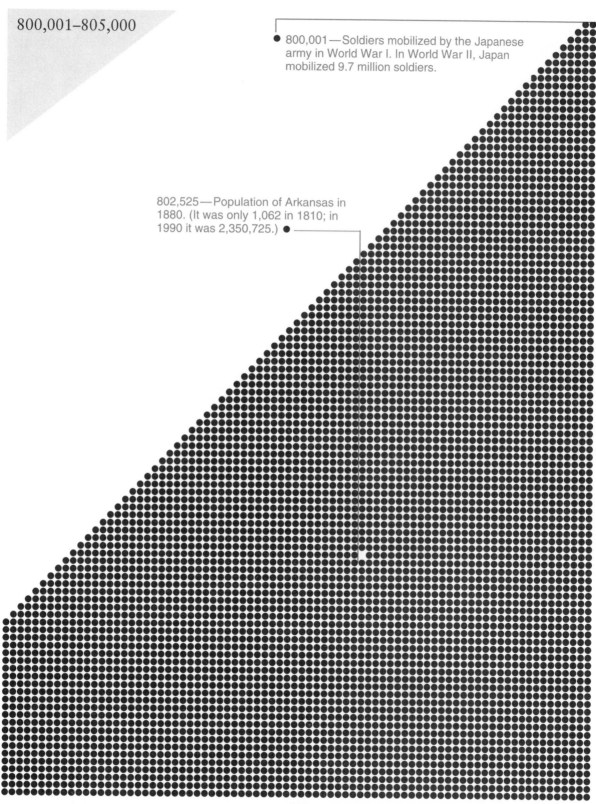

● 800,001—Soldiers mobilized by the Japanese army in World War I. In World War II, Japan mobilized 9.7 million soldiers.

802,525—Population of Arkansas in 1880. (It was only 1,062 in 1810; in 1990 it was 2,350,725.) ●

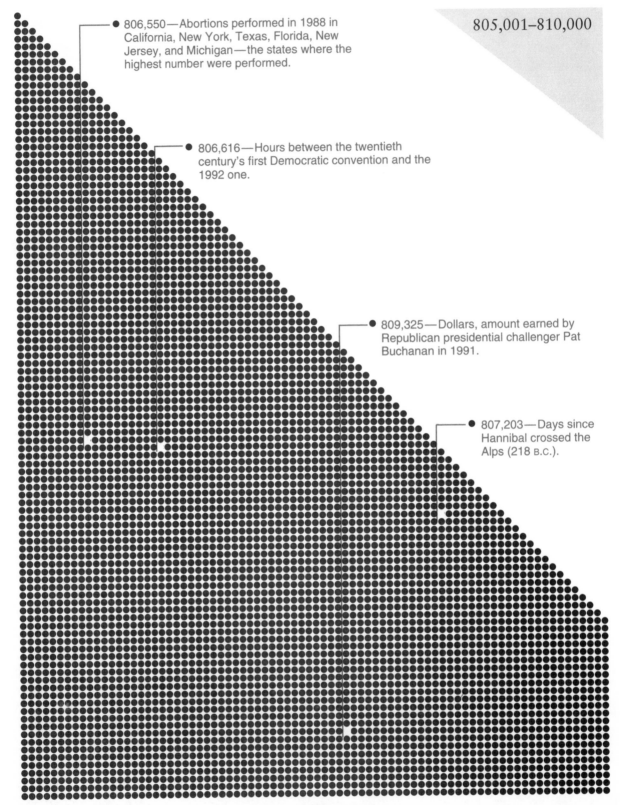

806,550—Abortions performed in 1988 in California, New York, Texas, Florida, New Jersey, and Michigan—the states where the highest number were performed.

806,616—Hours between the twentieth century's first Democratic convention and the 1992 one.

809,325—Dollars, amount earned by Republican presidential challenger Pat Buchanan in 1991.

807,203—Days since Hannibal crossed the Alps (218 B.C.).

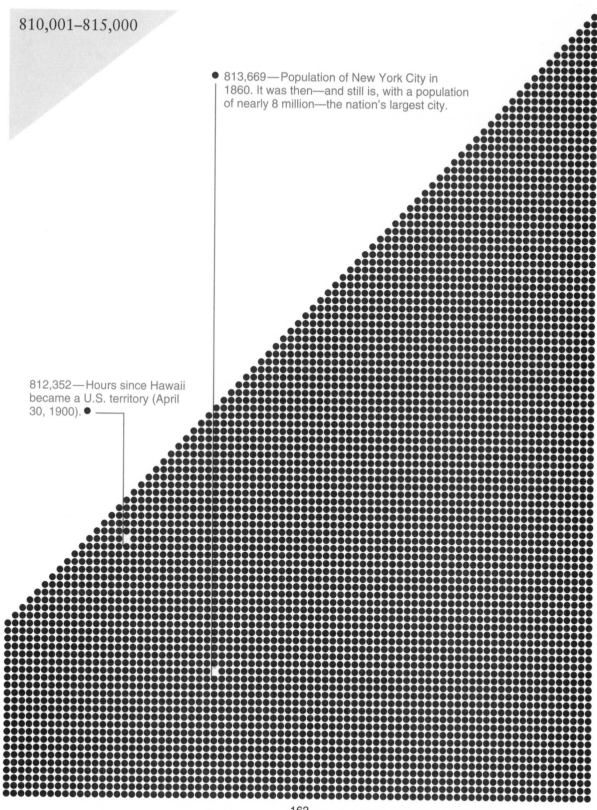

813,669—Population of New York City in 1860. It was then—and still is, with a population of nearly 8 million—the nation's largest city.

812,352—Hours since Hawaii became a U.S. territory (April 30, 1900).

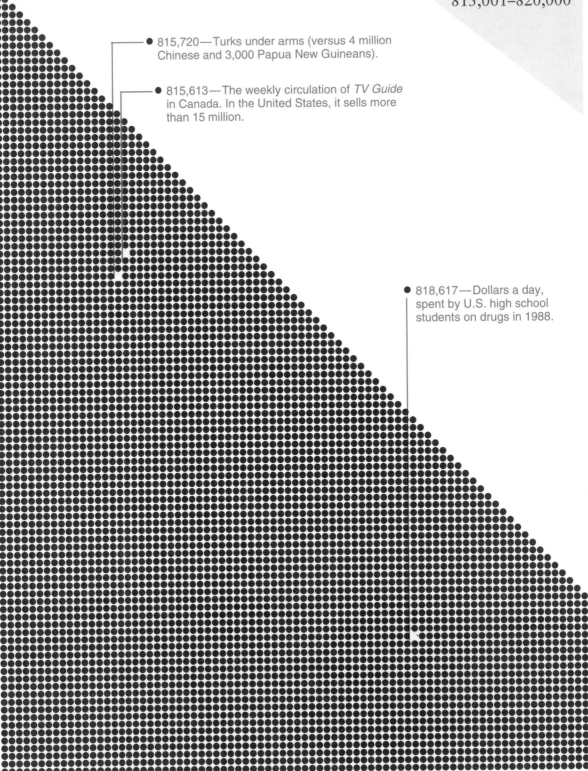

● 815,720—Turks under arms (versus 4 million
Chinese and 3,000 Papua New Guineans).

● 815,613—The weekly circulation of *TV Guide*
in Canada. In the United States, it sells more
than 15 million.

● 818,617—Dollars a day,
spent by U.S. high school
students on drugs in 1988.

820,788—Votes for candidates other than Bill Clinton, George Bush, and H. Ross Perot in 1992. This includes write-in votes in thirty-five states and D.C., and votes for "none of the above" in Nevada. ●

822,724—Eggs laid by American chickens every six minutes, 1990. ●

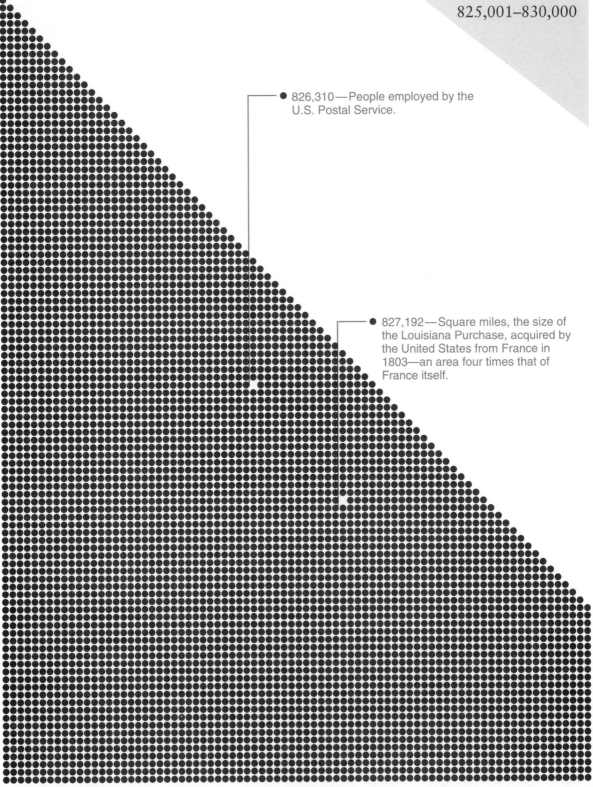

826,310—People employed by the U.S. Postal Service.

827,192—Square miles, the size of the Louisiana Purchase, acquired by the United States from France in 1803—an area four times that of France itself.

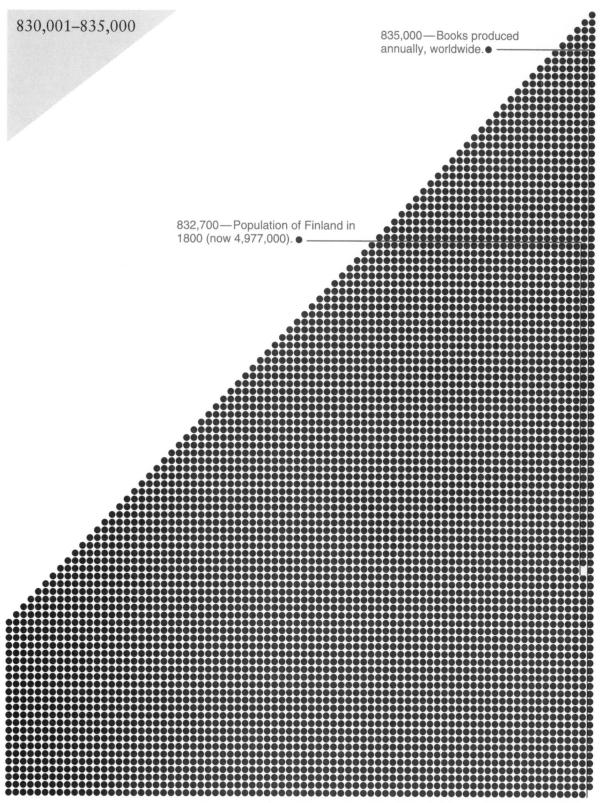

835,000—Books produced annually, worldwide.●

832,700—Population of Finland in 1800 (now 4,977,000).●

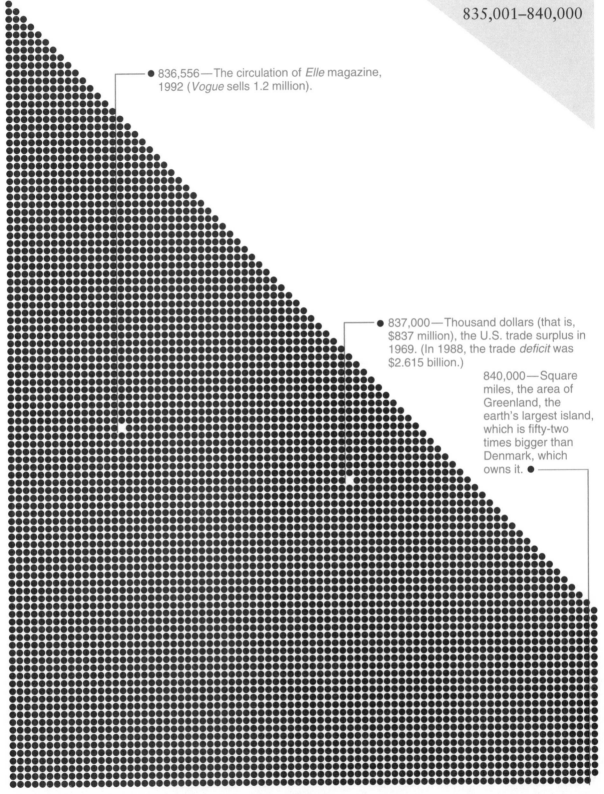

836,556—The circulation of *Elle* magazine, 1992 (*Vogue* sells 1.2 million).

837,000—Thousand dollars (that is, $837 million), the U.S. trade surplus in 1969. (In 1988, the trade *deficit* was $2.615 billion.)

840,000—Square miles, the area of Greenland, the earth's largest island, which is fifty-two times bigger than Denmark, which owns it. ●

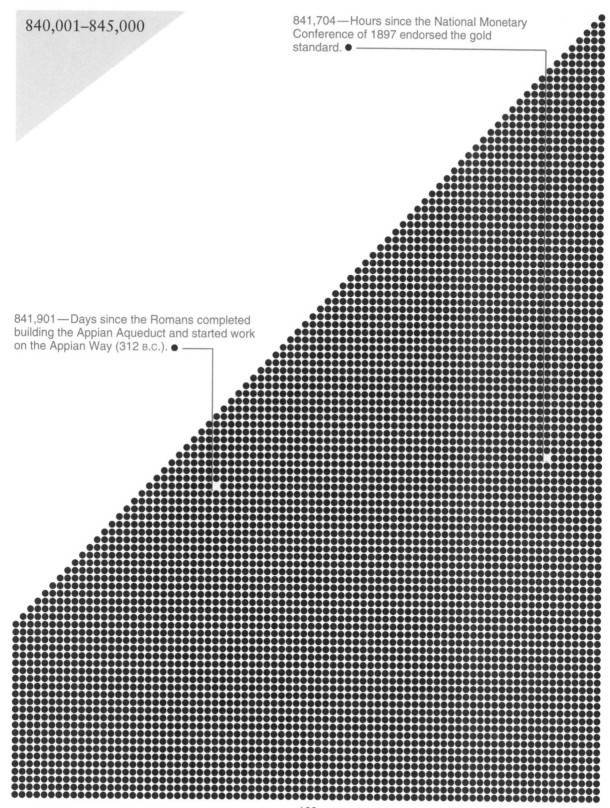

840,001–845,000

841,704—Hours since the National Monetary Conference of 1897 endorsed the gold standard. ●

841,901—Days since the Romans completed building the Appian Aqueduct and started work on the Appian Way (312 B.C.). ●

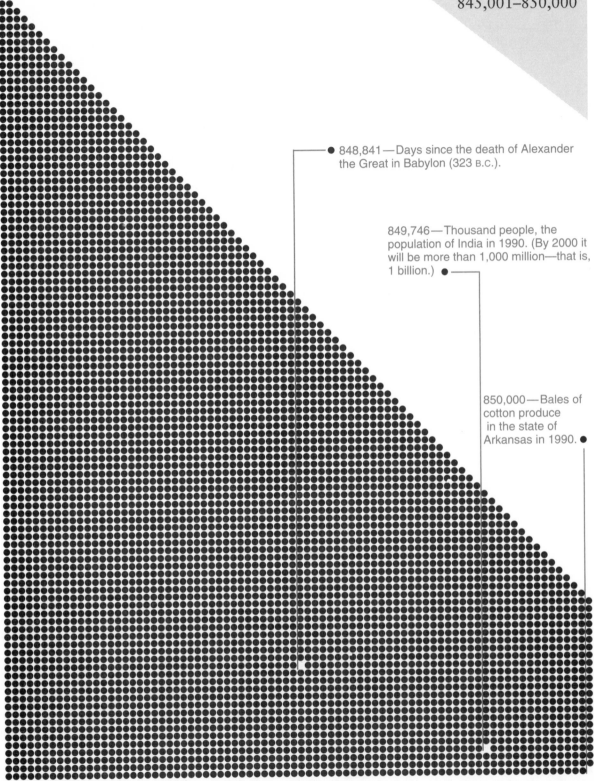

848,841—Days since the death of Alexander the Great in Babylon (323 B.C.).

849,746—Thousand people, the population of India in 1990. (By 2000 it will be more than 1,000 million—that is, 1 billion.)

850,000—Bales of cotton produce in the state of Arkansas in 1990.

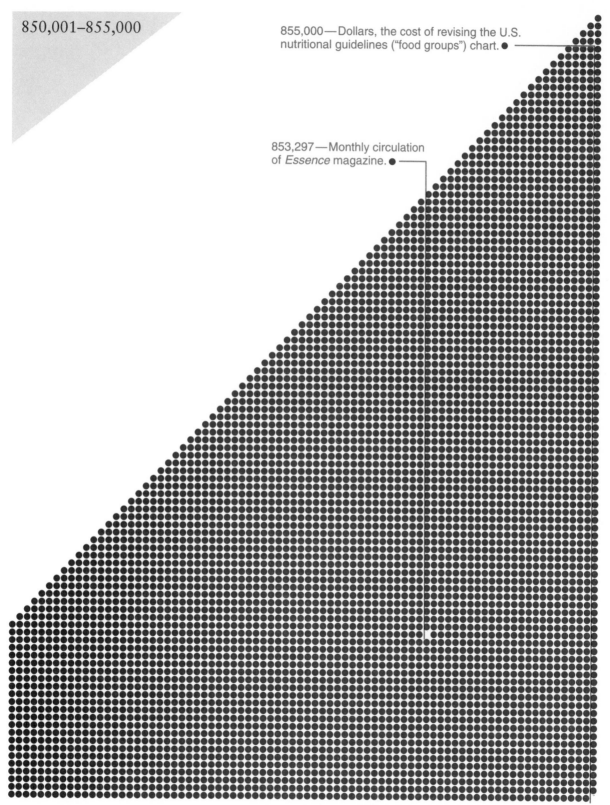

855,000—Dollars, the cost of revising the U.S. nutritional guidelines ("food groups") chart. ●

853,297—Monthly circulation of *Essence* magazine. ●

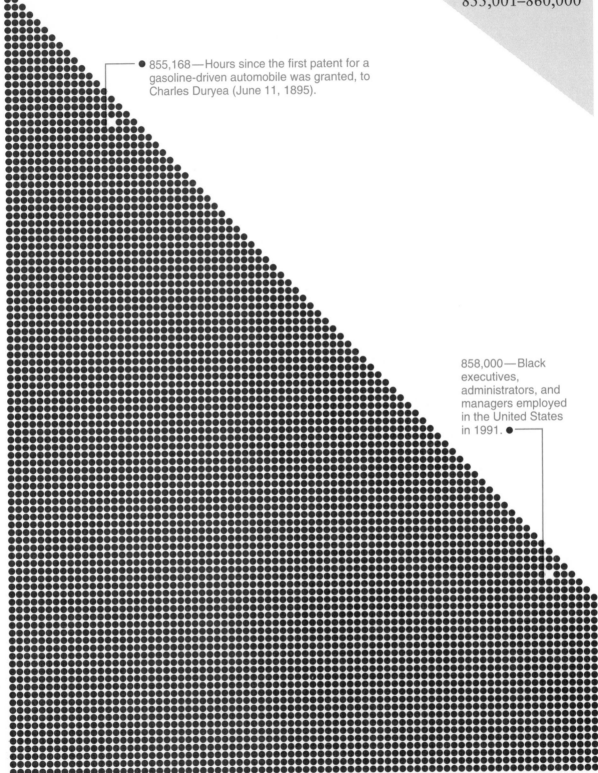

855,168—Hours since the first patent for a gasoline-driven automobile was granted, to Charles Duryea (June 11, 1895).

858,000—Black executives, administrators, and managers employed in the United States in 1991.

865,000—Days since Demosthenes
was a Greek orator. ●

862,076—Of every million people in the world
live in the Eastern Hemisphere. ●

861,500—American Indians live on
reservations, out of a total Native
American population of 1,534,000. ●

864,000—Miles, the
diameter of the Sun—
109 times the
diameter of the Earth. ●

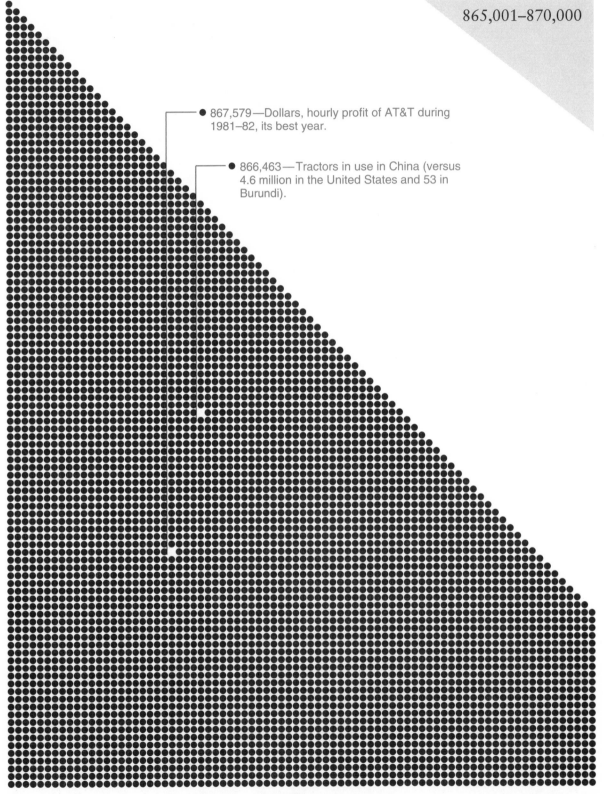

● 867,579—Dollars, hourly profit of AT&T during 1981–82, its best year.

● 866,463—Tractors in use in China (versus 4.6 million in the United States and 53 in Burundi).

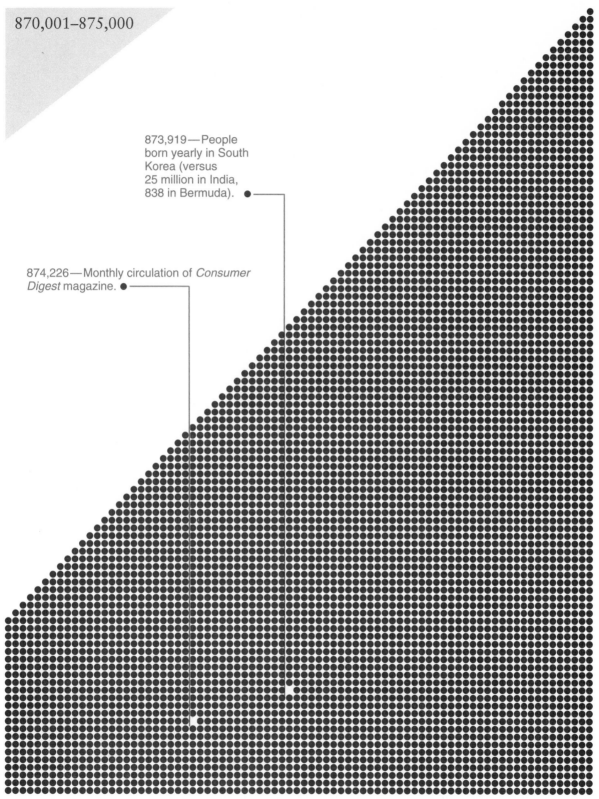

873,919—People born yearly in South Korea (versus 25 million in India, 838 in Bermuda). ●

874,226—Monthly circulation of *Consumer Digest* magazine. ●

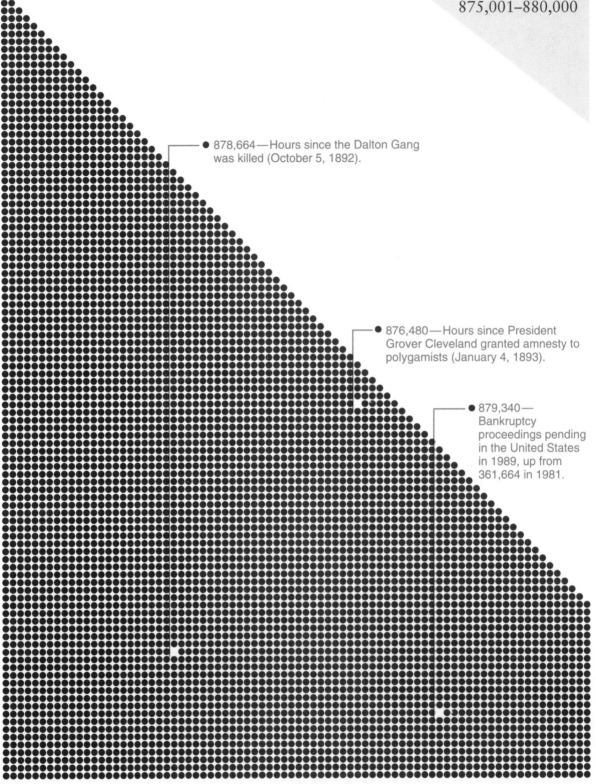

878,664—Hours since the Dalton Gang was killed (October 5, 1892).

876,480—Hours since President Grover Cleveland granted amnesty to polygamists (January 4, 1893).

879,340—Bankruptcy proceedings pending in the United States in 1989, up from 361,664 in 1981.

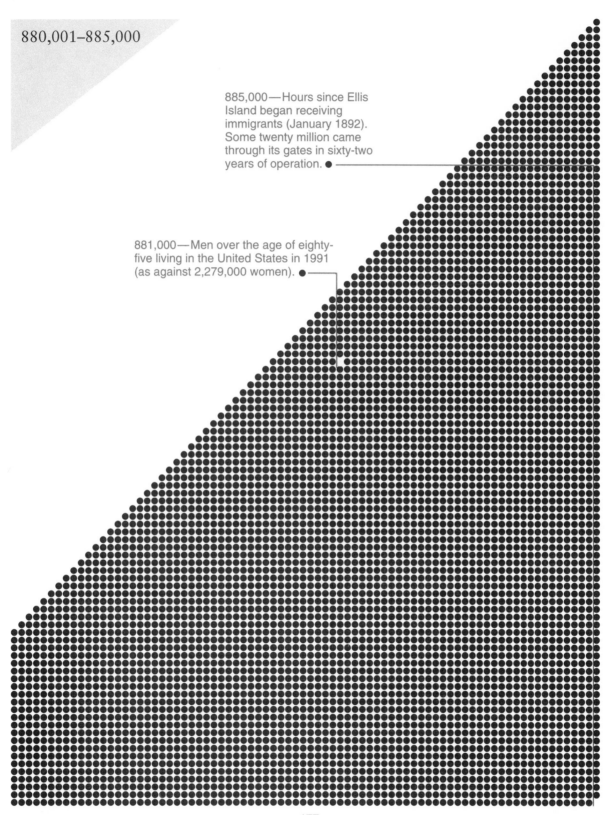

885,000—Hours since Ellis
Island began receiving
immigrants (January 1892).
Some twenty million came
through its gates in sixty-two
years of operation. ●———

881,000—Men over the age of eighty-
five living in the United States in 1991
(as against 2,279,000 women). ●

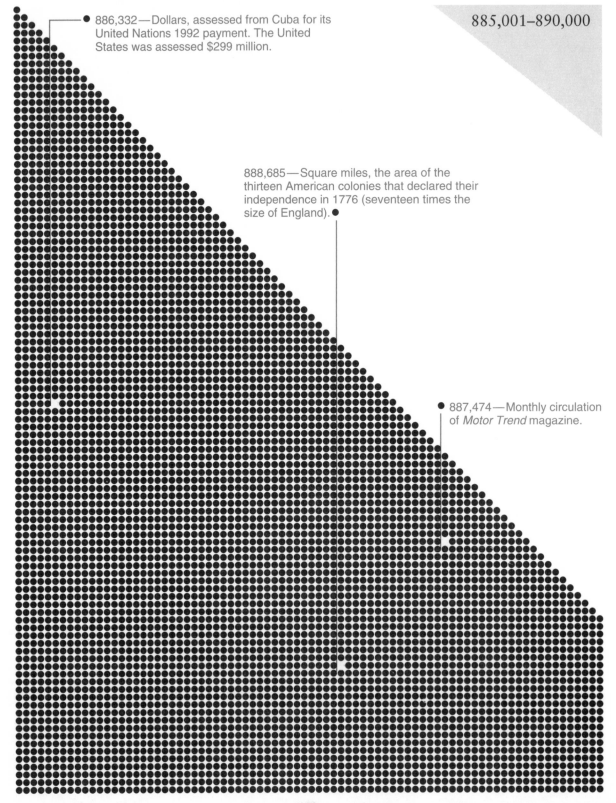

886,332—Dollars, assessed from Cuba for its United Nations 1992 payment. The United States was assessed $299 million.

888,685—Square miles, the area of the thirteen American colonies that declared their independence in 1776 (seventeen times the size of England).

887,474—Monthly circulation of *Motor Trend* magazine.

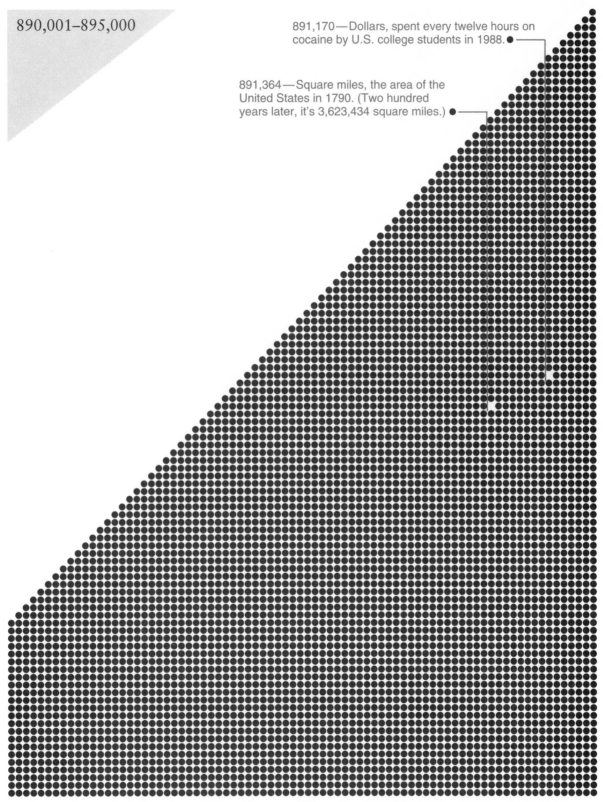

890,001–895,000

891,170—Dollars, spent every twelve hours on
cocaine by U.S. college students in 1988. ●

891,364—Square miles, the area of the
United States in 1790. (Two hundred
years later, it's 3,623,434 square miles.) ●

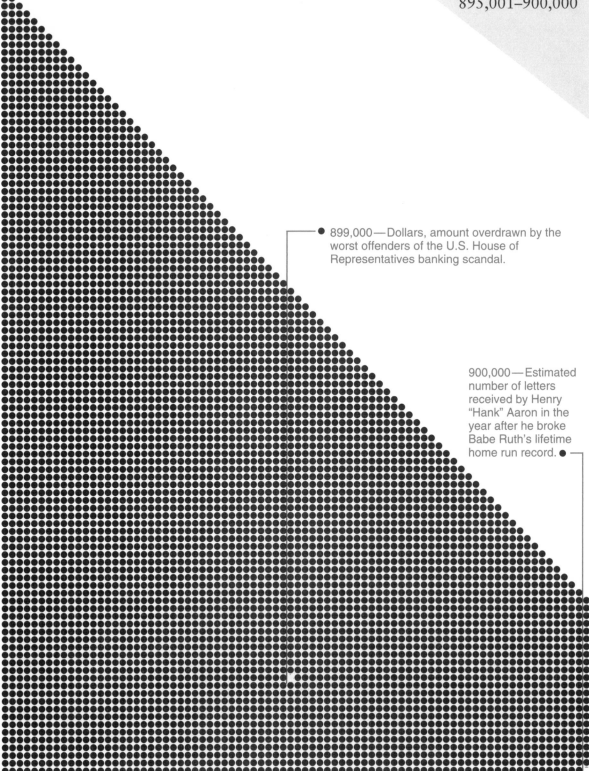

899,000—Dollars, amount overdrawn by the worst offenders of the U.S. House of Representatives banking scandal.

900,000—Estimated number of letters received by Henry "Hank" Aaron in the year after he broke Babe Ruth's lifetime home run record.

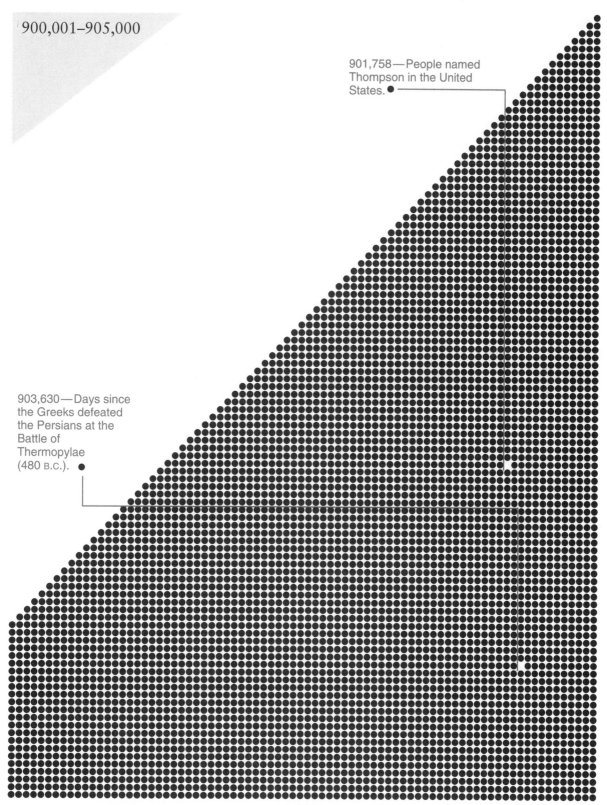

901,758—People named
Thompson in the United
States.

903,630—Days since
the Greeks defeated
the Persians at the
Battle of
Thermopylae
(480 B.C.).

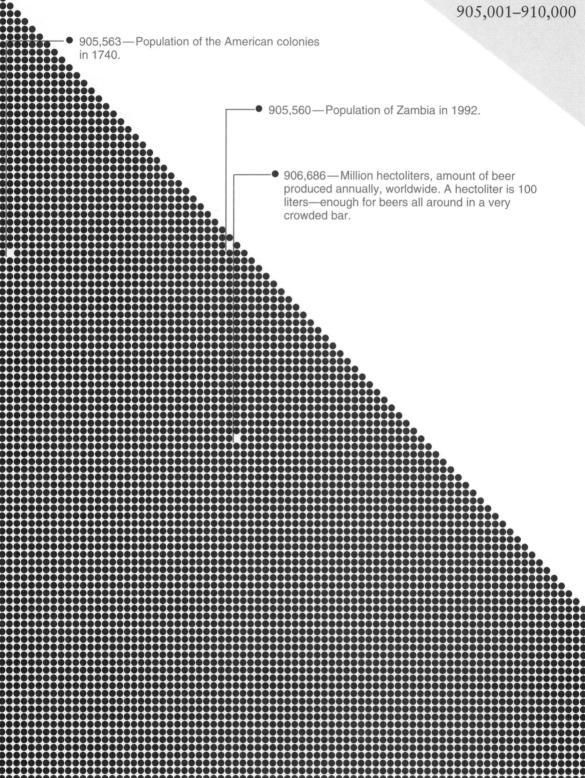

905,563—Population of the American colonies in 1740.

905,560—Population of Zambia in 1992.

906,686—Million hectoliters, amount of beer produced annually, worldwide. A hectoliter is 100 liters—enough for beers all around in a very crowded bar.

910,758—Horses in India (versus 10.9 million in China, 1,000 in Sri Lanka). ●

912,673—97×97×97. ●

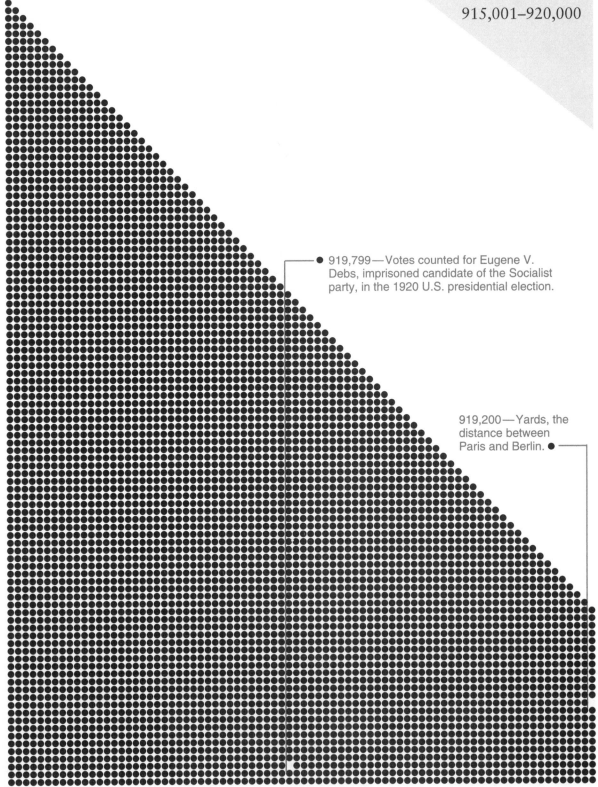

919,799—Votes counted for Eugene V. Debs, imprisoned candidate of the Socialist party, in the 1920 U.S. presidential election.

919,200—Yards, the distance between Paris and Berlin.

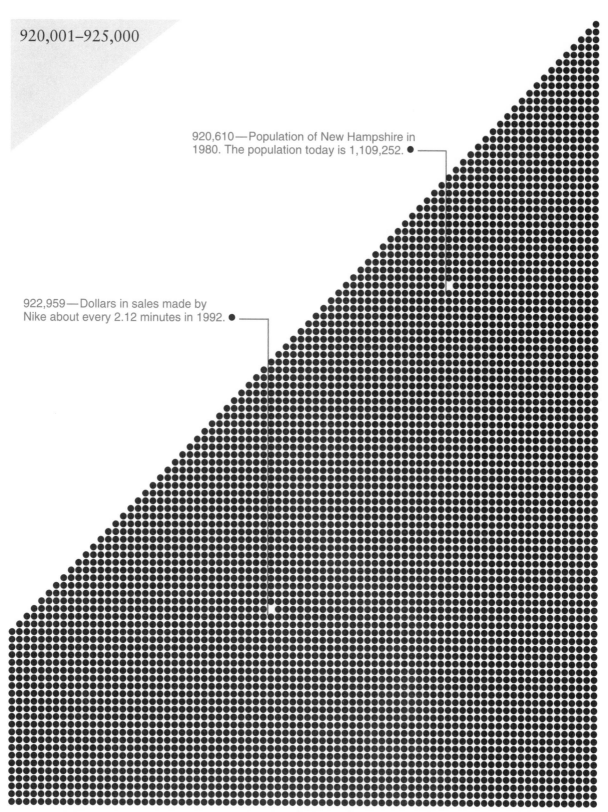

920,001–925,000

920,610—Population of New Hampshire in
1980. The population today is 1,109,252. ●

922,959—Dollars in sales made by
Nike about every 2.12 minutes in 1992. ●

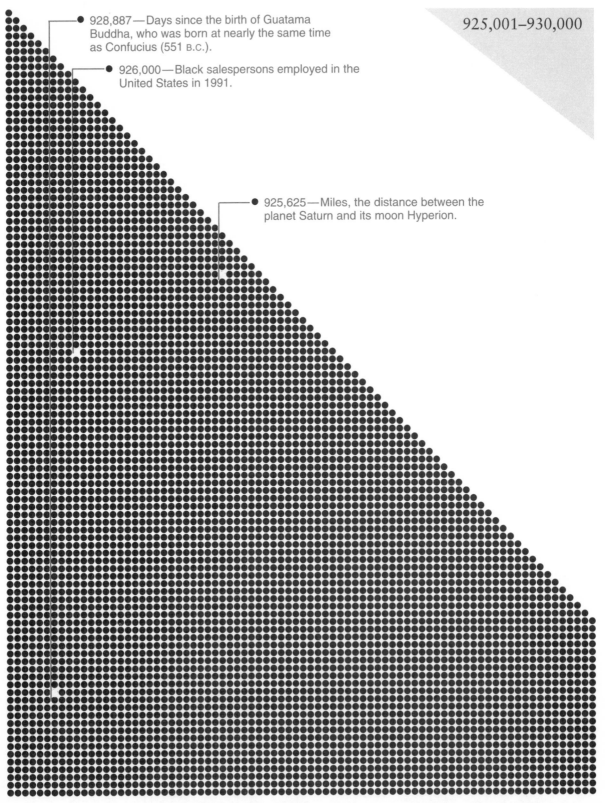

928,887—Days since the birth of Guatama Buddha, who was born at nearly the same time as Confucius (551 B.C.).

926,000—Black salespersons employed in the United States in 1991.

925,625—Miles, the distance between the planet Saturn and its moon Hyperion.

930,001–935,000

935,000—Dollars earned by the state of
Vermont through liquor sales. The combined
revenue of the seventeen states that operate a
liquor monopoly was $502,798,000. ●

934,943—Population of the state of Maryland
in 1880 (now 4.78 million). ●

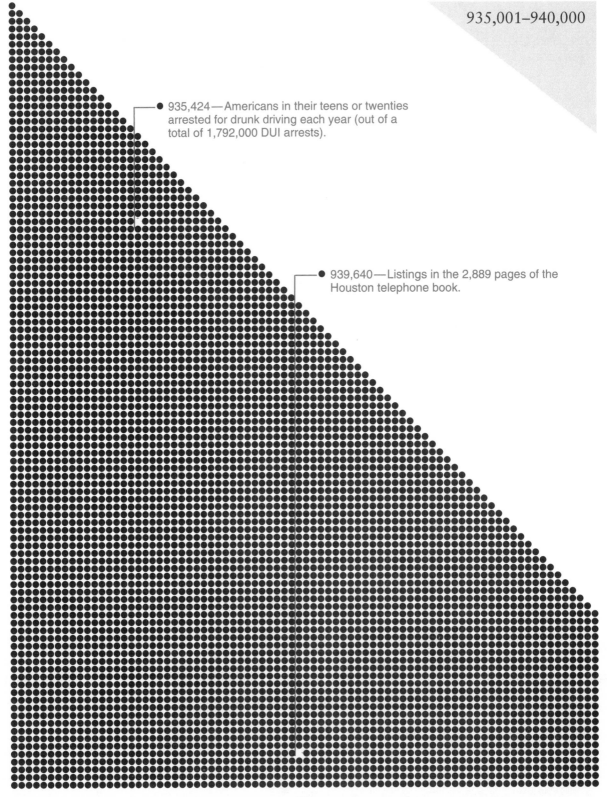

935,424—Americans in their teens or twenties arrested for drunk driving each year (out of a total of 1,792,000 DUI arrests).

939,640—Listings in the 2,889 pages of the Houston telephone book.

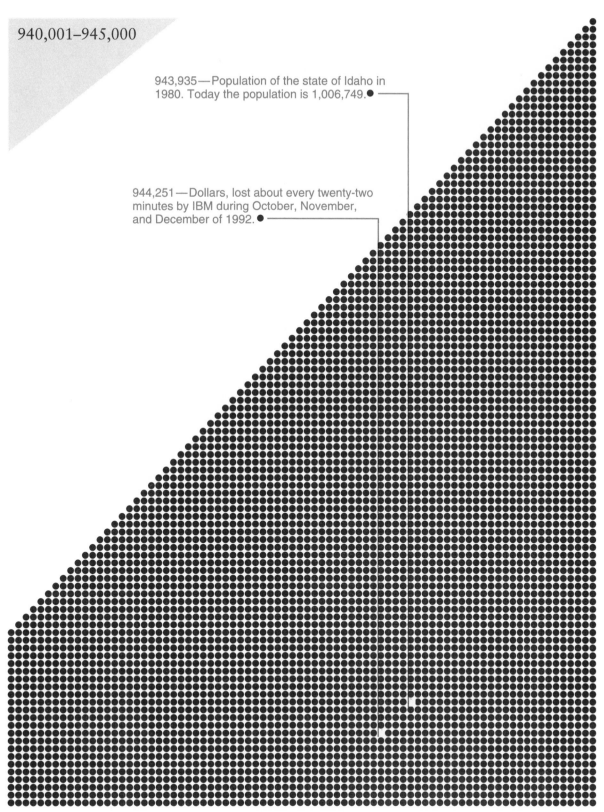

943,935—Population of the state of Idaho in
1980. Today the population is 1,006,749.●

944,251—Dollars, lost about every twenty-two
minutes by IBM during October, November,
and December of 1992. ●

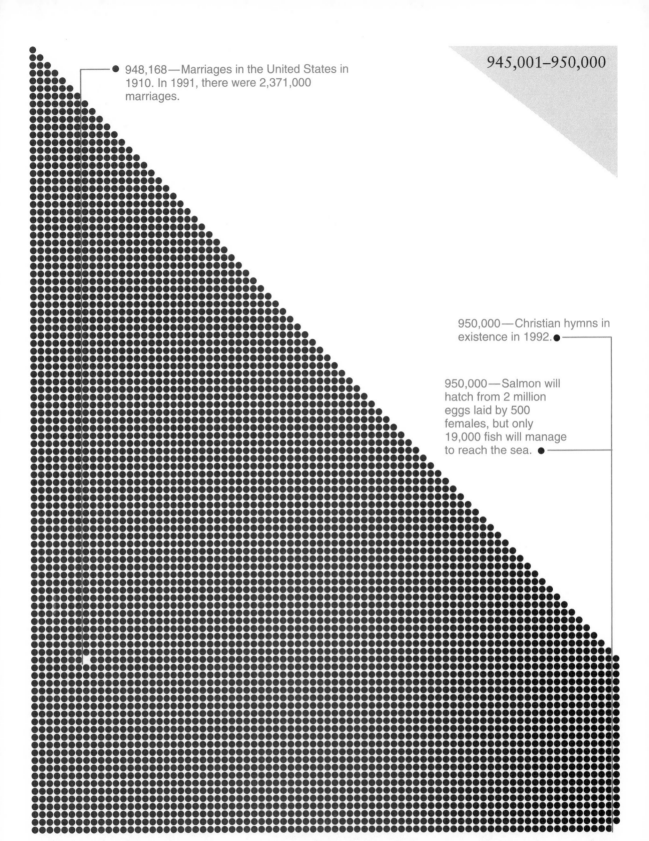

948,168—Marriages in the United States in 1910. In 1991, there were 2,371,000 marriages.

950,000—Christian hymns in existence in 1992.

950,000—Salmon will hatch from 2 million eggs laid by 500 females, but only 19,000 fish will manage to reach the sea.

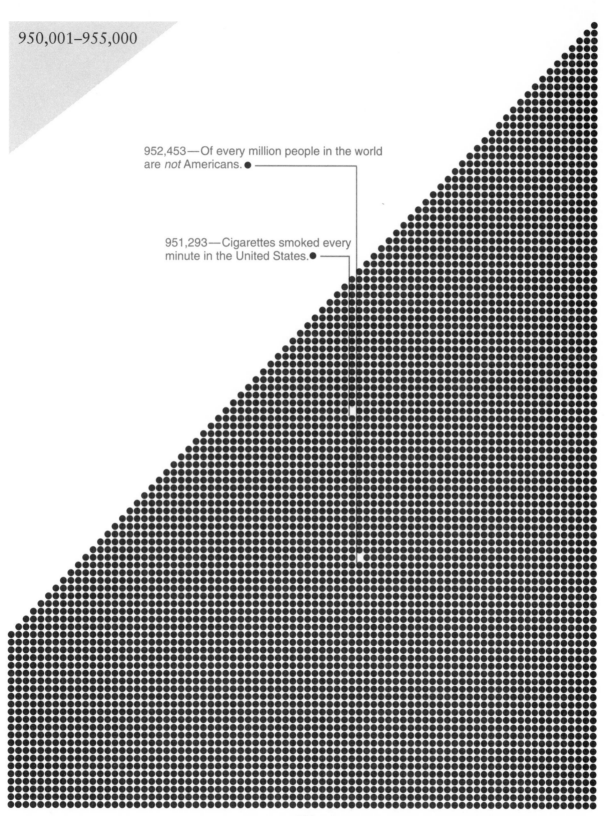

950,001–955,000

952,453—Of every million people in the world
are *not* Americans. ●

951,293—Cigarettes smoked every
minute in the United States. ●

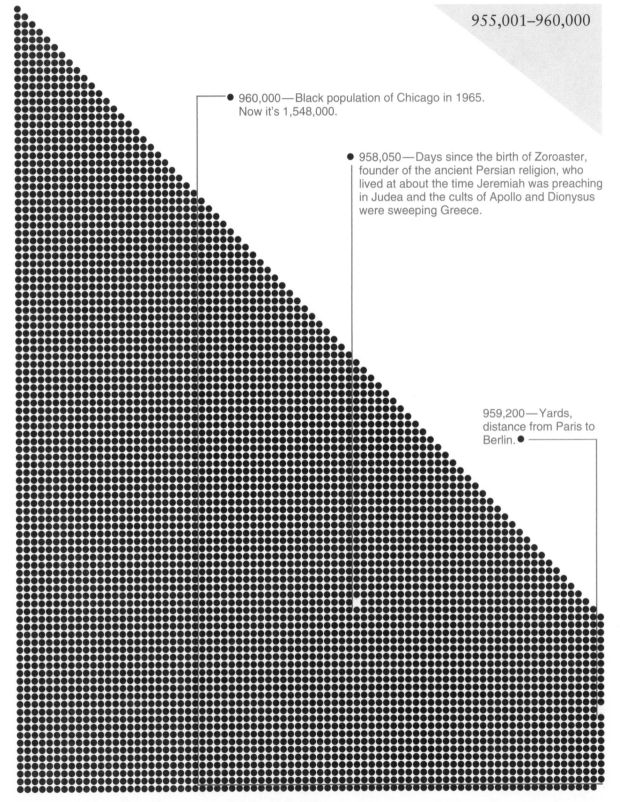

960,000—Black population of Chicago in 1965. Now it's 1,548,000.

958,050—Days since the birth of Zoroaster, founder of the ancient Persian religion, who lived at about the time Jeremiah was preaching in Judea and the cults of Apollo and Dionysus were sweeping Greece.

959,200—Yards, distance from Paris to Berlin.

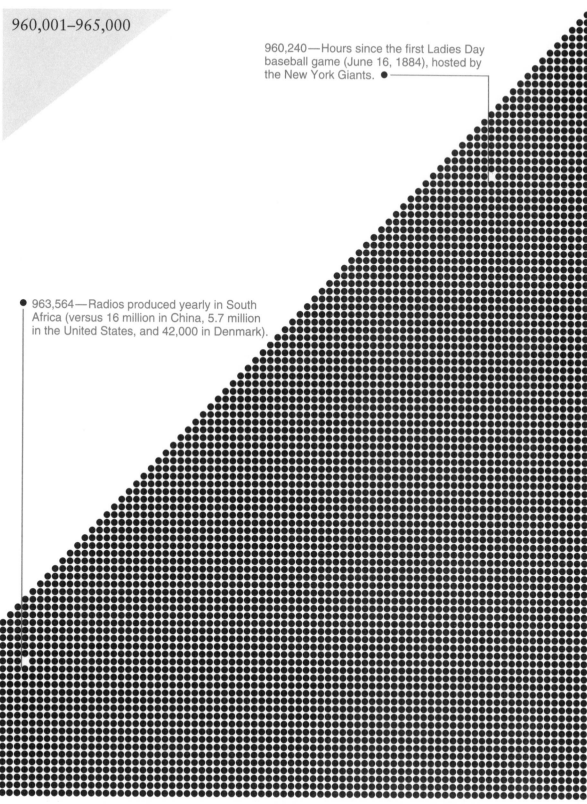

960,240—Hours since the first Ladies Day baseball game (June 16, 1884), hosted by the New York Giants. ●

963,564—Radios produced yearly in South Africa (versus 16 million in China, 5.7 million in the United States, and 42,000 in Denmark).

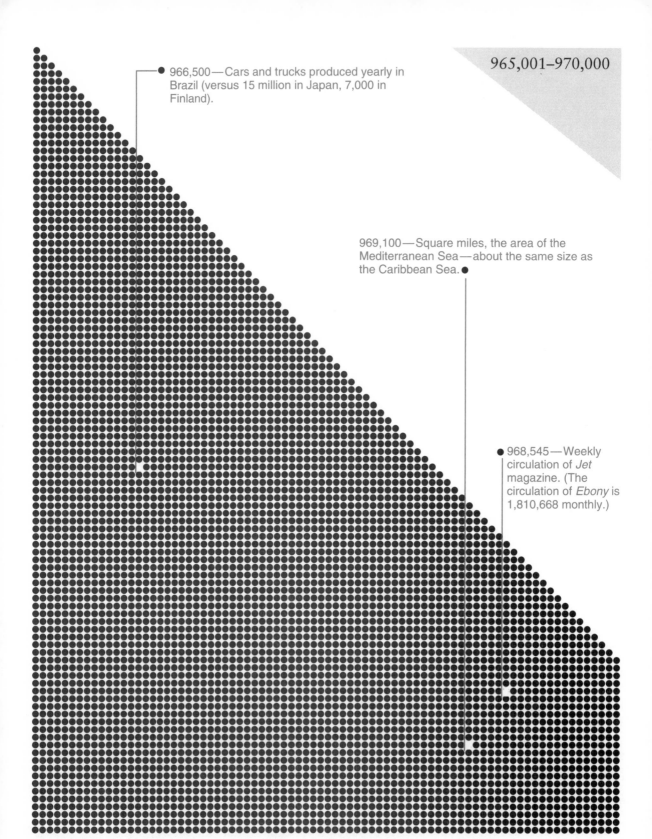

966,500—Cars and trucks produced yearly in Brazil (versus 15 million in Japan, 7,000 in Finland).

969,100—Square miles, the area of the Mediterranean Sea—about the same size as the Caribbean Sea.

968,545—Weekly circulation of *Jet* magazine. (The circulation of *Ebony* is 1,810,668 monthly.)

972,533—Americans named Moore. ●

974,731—To 1, the odds against dying a
nonviolent death, if you are a codfish.●

971,000—Square miles, the area of the
Sahara Desert's 3.5 million square
miles that is covered by sand dunes.●

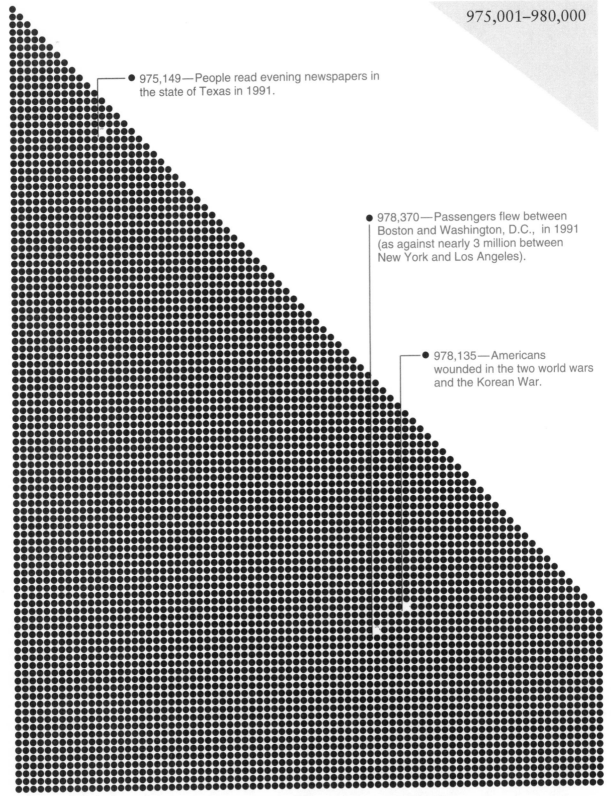

975,149—People read evening newspapers in
the state of Texas in 1991.

978,370—Passengers flew between
Boston and Washington, D.C., in 1991
(as against nearly 3 million between
New York and Los Angeles).

978,135—Americans
wounded in the two world wars
and the Korean War.

983,796—Dollars, amount earned every fifteen minutes by U.S. banks between July and September of 1992. ●

984,736—Miles of road in Brazil (versus 3.9 million in the United States, 187,223 in Italy, and 45 in the Falkland Islands). ●

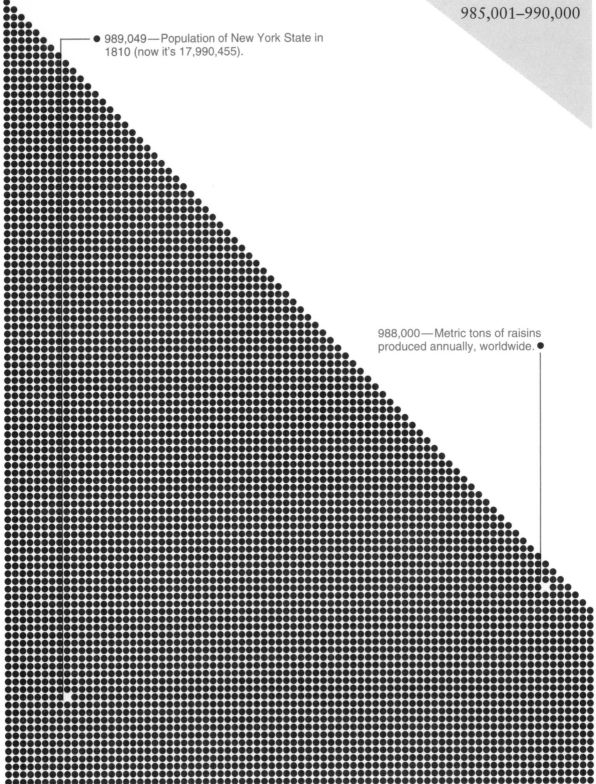

● 989,049—Population of New York State in 1810 (now it's 17,990,455).

988,000—Metric tons of raisins produced annually, worldwide. ●

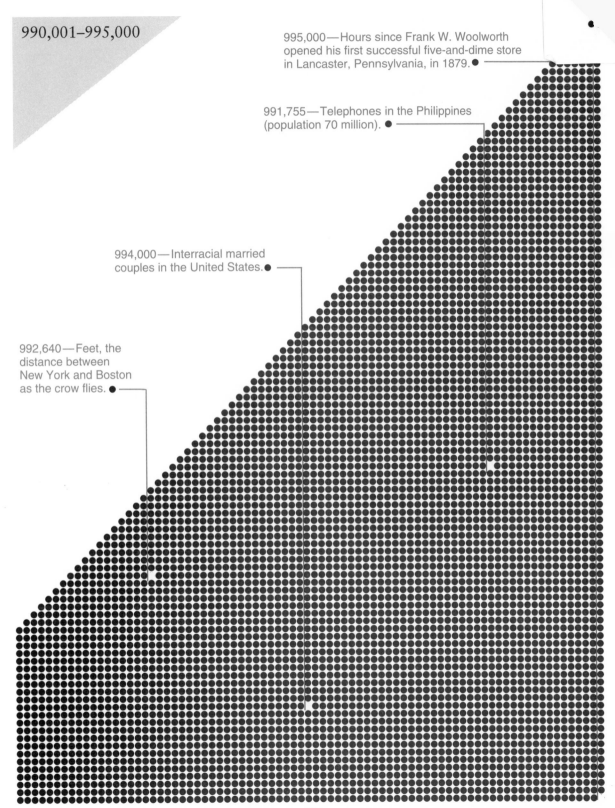

995,000—Hours since Frank W. Woolworth opened his first successful five-and-dime store in Lancaster, Pennsylvania, in 1879. ●

991,755—Telephones in the Philippines (population 70 million). ●

994,000—Interracial married couples in the United States. ●

992,640—Feet, the distance between New York and Boston as the crow flies. ●

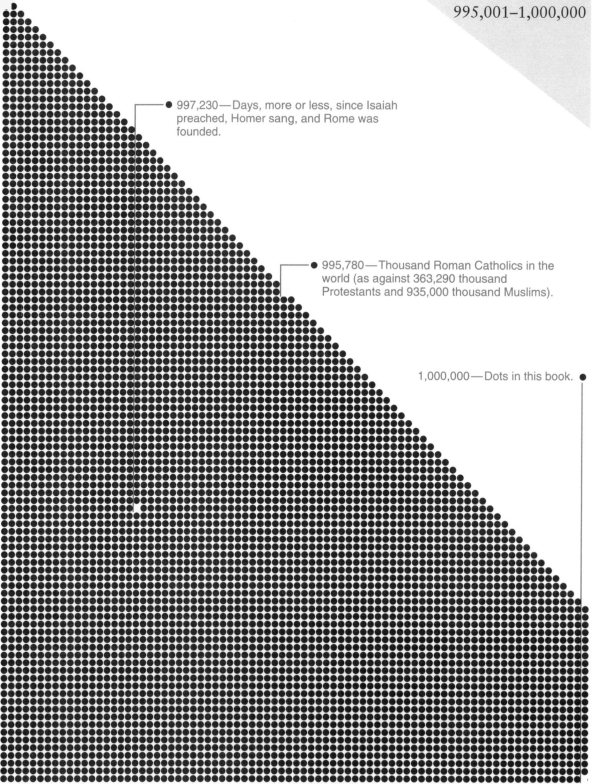

997,230—Days, more or less, since Isaiah preached, Homer sang, and Rome was founded.

995,780—Thousand Roman Catholics in the world (as against 363,290 thousand Protestants and 935,000 thousand Muslims).

1,000,000—Dots in this book.

About the Author

HENDRIK HERTZBERG became executive editor of *The New Yorker,* where he had been a staff writer from 1969 to 1977, in September 1992. From 1981 to 1992 he was associated with *The New Republic* as editor, national political correspondent, and editor again. He served on the White House staff during the whole of the Carter administration and was President Carter's chief speech writer during his last two years in office. A native of New York, Mr. Hertzberg is a graduate of Harvard and a veteran of the U.S. Navy.